To 1

MW01231899

DISCOVERING CARL SANDBURG

The *Eclectic Life* of an *American Icon*

BIOGRAPHER • JOURNALIST • CELEBRITY

CHILDREN'S AUTHOR • POET OF THE PEOPLE

ORATOR • NOVELIST • LINCOLN HISTORIAN

FOLKLORIST AND SINGER • SOCIAL ACTIVIST

JOHN W. QUINLEY

Help others discover...

John W. Quinley

Published by:
Mt. Camp Books
HENDERSONVILLE, NC

ISBN: 979-8-218-05120-4

COVER PHOTO: Carl Sandburg as a young man in 1893. Used with permission of the Rare Book & Manuscript Library, University of Illinois, Urbana-Champaign

Typesetting and cover by Gary A. Rosenberg
www.thebookcouple.com

Printed in the United States of America

To my wife, Melissa Quinley

*During my years studying Carl Sandburg,
she listened to countless stories, reviewed articles
and chapters, and made insightful editorial
suggestions. When I struggled with the research
and writing, she encouraged me to see it to the
end. There would be no book without her.*

Contents

Foreword

We Sandburg enthusiasts who have visited his humble three-room birthplace cottage in Galesburg, Illinois, and learned about his hardscrabble youth and uneven formal education are astonished at the breadth and depth of his accomplishments. By the end of his extraordinary life, Carl Sandburg was acclaimed throughout the world. In his fine book *Discovering Carl Sandburg: The Eclectic Life of an American Icon,* author Dr. John W. Quinley delves into Sandburg the biographer, social activist, poet of the people, journalist, orator, performer, folklorist, children's author, Lincoln historian, novelist, film critic, and celebrity. In his engaging book, Dr. Quinley explains why Sandburg should be viewed as an American icon. The book includes an extensive bibliography with works by and about Sandburg that readers can consult to learn more about this eclectic man.

Sandburg's hero was Abraham Lincoln. Both men faced daunting challenges in their youth. At an early age both men developed an insatiable appetite for learning. Both learned about the power of the written and spoken word. Both excelled at putting these powers to good use. Sandburg studied Lincoln exhaustively for many years. A case could be made that Sandburg understood the sixteenth president better than any other man or woman.

Lincoln and Sandburg had a deep, abiding concern for the working class. Lincoln worked as an Illinois state legislator to improve the lot of the working class by sponsoring internal improvements. As president he signed the Homestead Act of 1862, which gave settlers opportunities during the westward expansion. He signed land-grant legislation, which led to the creation of public universities. Sandburg fervently worked for the working class as an organizer for the Social-Democratic Party of Wisconsin as a young man. In his epic book-length poem *The People, Yes* written during the depth of the Great Depression, Sandburg affirms the will of the American people to survive much as John Steinbeck did in *The Grapes of Wrath*:

> The people will live on.
> The learning and blundering people will live on.
> They will be tricked and sold and again sold
> And go back to the nourishing earth for rootholds,
> The people so peculiar in renewal and comeback,
> You can't laugh off their capacity to take it.

A North Carolina state official assessed the breadth and depth of Sandburg's accomplishments at a ceremony welcoming the Sandburg family to Connemara in the 1940s. He placed Sandburg in lofty company. He remarked:

> Our guest of honor Carl Sandburg is an original-something that has never happened before. Something new under the sun. And how does this come about? Those schooled in science might call it a mutation! Those steeped in religion will call it a miracle. . . . Surely free-swinging Walt Whitman

was his great-uncle and shy, sensitive Emily Dickinson was his great-aunt.

Among his distant relatives I find Bret Harte and Mark Twain, while his first cousins could be Vachel Lindsay, Edgar Lee Masters, and Robert Frost, and I think among his nephews we might even find our own Thomas Wolfe. But when I come to name his literary father, I hesitate and then go on to say that he could have been that tall, angular man with the stovepipe hat who went to Gettysburg one day and made a brief, immortal address. And if I were so bold as to attempt to name his spiritual ancestor, I would suggest that patriarch whose gifted hand wrote the book of Job.

Dr. Quinley ably covers the breadth and depth of Sandburg's accomplishments. Readers of *Discovering Carl Sandburg* will learn why he should be considered an American icon.

—Michael Hobbs, April 2022
Member of Carl Sandburg Historic Site Association
Board of Directors, Galesburg, IL, and editor of
its quarterly newsletter, *Inklings and Idlings*

Introduction

During the first half of the twentieth century, Carl Sandburg seemed to be everywhere and do everything: poet and political activist; investigative reporter, columnist, and film critic; lecturer, folk singer, and musicologist; Lincoln biographer and historian; children's author; novelist; and media celebrity. He was one of the most successful American writers of the twentieth century. Everyone knew his name. But as time went on, his fame began to fade, and by the twenty-first century, the public knew little, if anything, about his legacy.

Like so many of my generation, I was introduced to Sandburg's iconic poems "Chicago" and "Fog" as a high school student during the 1950s, but that was the extent of my knowledge. Nearly sixty years later, I was given the chance to take college students to visit the Carl Sandburg Home Historic Site in western North Carolina. In preparation for the visit, I read a biographical essay written by Sandburg's granddaughter. My education continued when I became a volunteer at the Home. I read the docent guide prepared by the park rangers, and most of the more than thirty books Sandburg had written, and nearly three dozen books and articles that others wrote about him. Over several years, my thirty-minute tours led to longer presentations at other venues, an article on the Sandburg Home website, articles for *Inklings and Idlings* (the newsletter of the Carl Sandburg Historic Site Association in Galesburg, Illinois), and eventually to my writing this book.

Visitors to the Home are amazed to learn about Sandburg's eclectic life and works, and some ask what they could read to learn more. Although there are two autobiographies, ten biographies, three memoirs, and nine books written about specific aspects of the Sandburg legacy, there is little readily available today and nothing is recent. As a tour guide, I routinely recommend the park handbook as well as *Carl Sandburg: A Biography* written by Penelope Niven in 1991, but no one on my tours buys the book when they realize it is 800-plus pages.

This slim book fills the gap for a new generation of readers. It is organized into thirteen chapters that discuss areas of Sandburg's achievements or touch upon aspects of his personal life, such as his wife's world-famous goats. Each chapter provides historical context, anecdotes, quotations from poetry and prose, and quotations from authors who have written about Sandburg.

Sandburg deserves to regain his place in American culture, and readers will see how issues of social justice addressed by Sandburg in the twentieth century (e.g., disparity of incomes, racial injustices, dangers of propaganda) are relevant today. It is my wish that this book will help readers discover—or rediscover—this remarkable American icon.

Chapter One

Foundations
of an American Icon

Sandburg visited his hometown of Galesburg, Illinois, in 1951 to gather and confirm memories from relatives and boyhood friends about his early life. They recalled the antics of the gang of neighborhood boys, "The Dirty Dozen," who enjoyed playing baseball, hanging around the courthouse to hear trials, and playing music. In particular, they recalled one unforgettable day the gang sat for hours in the city jail after being arrested for swimming naked in a pond inside the city limits. Sandburg published his autobiography about these early days, titled *Always the Young Strangers* in 1953, on his seventy-fifth birthday.

Sandburg biographer Penelope Niven described the book as a "forthright narrative of his boyhood as a discerningly universal story of coming-of-age."[1] Reviews in the *New York Times* and the *Christian Science Monitor* concluded the book was "the best autobiography ever written by an American" and "might well prove to be the best beloved of all American biographies."[2]

Always the Young Strangers portrays a stable boyhood of small-town life largely before industrialization transformed the late nineteenth century. Sandburg grew up in a large, working-class family in a town of 15,000 people, where many were foreign born—like the Swedish Sandburgs—and most worked for the railroad. But the town didn't lack sophisticated culture. Called the "Athens of the Corn Belt," it had two small liberal arts colleges (Lombard and Knox) and a business school. And as a major hub for the railroad, the town routinely drew in vaudeville entertainers, politicians, opera stars, magicians, circuses, evangelists, and more.

Hardworking and frugal, Sandburg's father, August Sandburg, was a blacksmith's helper who worked long hours on steam locomotives. When the first cold days of winter came, he would nurse a pint of pure grain alcohol until spring by occasionally spooning a little into his coffee. Although he seldom read and never learned to write in English, he was no fool. He patiently saved up enough money to buy a ten-room house, rented out four rooms, and maintained the property himself. Sandburg writes in *Always the Young Strangers*:

> The ten-room house on Berrien Street was a challenge to August Sandburg. He couldn't see himself paying—or wasting—money for repairs. He became a carpenter, a bricklayer, a house painter, a paperhanger, a cabinetmaker, a truck gardener, a handyman restless and dissatisfied unless there was something to fix or improve on the property he owned or was paying for. What he made or fixed with his hands wasn't always finished perfectly smooth and correct—but it would do, it would serve. I was his helper, his chore boy, my brother Mart later throwing in.[3]

Sandburg's mother, Clara Mathilda, kept the large family together and encouraged the children's interest in learning. His four siblings who reached adulthood became a schoolteacher, a music teacher, a nurse and a schoolteacher, and a white-collar employee in business and government. None made a living with their hands.

As a boy of eleven, Sandburg cleaned offices and delivered newspapers, and after eighth grade, a severe national economic depression compelled him to work full-time. He worked jobs ranging from delivering milk and milking cows to laboring in a brickyard and icehouse, harvesting wheat, and renting out rowboats at a local lake. Most of the jobs were of short duration and required manual labor—all were dead-end. Although Sandburg never attended high school, he read all his sister's high school books. In 1963, on his eighty-fifth birthday, Galesburg High awarded him an honorary diploma.

Sandburg came to know most of the people in the town, "from the most respected to the most flagrantly immoral and the laziest, no-account bum."[4] He writes about how these early experiences helped shape his poetic vision:

> In those years as a boy in that prairie town I got education in scraps and pieces of many kinds, not knowing that they were part of my education. I met people in Galesburg who were puzzling to me, and later when I read Shakespeare, I found those same people were puzzling him. I met little wonders of many kinds among animals and plants that never lost their wonder for me, and I found later that these same wonders had a deep interest for Emerson, Thoreau, and Walt Whitman. I met

superstitions, folk's tales, and folklore while I was a young spalpeen, "a broth of a boy" long before I read books about them. All had their part, small or large, in the education I got outside of books and schools.[5]

For most of his teenage years, Sandburg stayed close to home. When he was sixteen, he took the train to nearby Peoria for a day at the State Fair. At eighteen, he traveled to Chicago for three days, living cheap with only one dollar and fifty cents in his pockets. At nineteen, he left home and joined the tens of thousands of men escaping the Panic of 1893 as hobos. Sandburg wrote in his first autobiography, *Always the Young Strangers*:

> Now I would take to the Road, see rivers and mountains, every day meeting strangers to whom I was one more young stranger. My family didn't like the idea. Papa scowled. Mamma kissed me and her eyes had tears after dinner one noon when I walked out of the house with my hands free, no bag or bundle, wearing a black-sateen shirt, coat, vest, and pants, a slouch hat, good shoes and socks, no underwear, in my pockets a small bar of soap, a razor, a comb, a pocket mirror, two handkerchiefs, a piece of string, needles and thread, a Waterbury watch, a knife, a pipe and a sack of tobacco, three dollars and twenty-five cents in cash.[6]

He traveled to Iowa, Nebraska, Colorado, Kansas, Missouri, and back—2,000 miles in four months. He threshed wheat, harvested hay, washed dishes, worked on a railroad gang, and chopped wood. Flophouses, barn lofts, and hobo jungles sheltered him, and ragged bands of hobos welcomed him into their rough kind of community. His horizons were expanding both geographically and intellectually. Sandburg said:

> I was meeting fellow travelers and fellow Americans. What they were doing to my heart and mind, my personality, I couldn't say then nor later and be certain. I was getting a deeper self-respect than I had had in Galesburg, so much I knew. I was getting to be a better storyteller. You can be loose and easy when from day to day you meet strangers you will know only an hour or a day or two. . . .[7]
>
> Away deep in my heart now I had hope as never before. Struggles lay ahead, I was sure, but whatever they were I would not be afraid of them.[8]

Biographer Harry Golden writes in *Carl Sandburg* that from this point forward, Sandburg embraced a life of "not always knowing the how's and where's, but perennially traveling, seeking, and experimenting."[9] In "The Road and the End," published in Sandburg's first book of poetry, *Chicago Poems*, he envisages:

> I shall foot it
> Down the roadway in the dusk,
> Where the shapes of hunger wander
> And the fugitives of pain go by . . .
>
> Regret shall be the gravel under foot . . .
> The dust of the traveled road
> Shall touch my hands and face.[10]

College Years

Sandburg chronicles his college years and early adulthood in a second autobiography, *Ever the Winds of Chance*. He finished only a detailed core sketch of the book, which was published posthumously in 1983, edited by eldest daughter, Margaret. He writes about his part-time jobs as a bell ringer and call man (firefighter) while attending Lombard College, as well as his teachers, classmates, and classes and his experiences in college life—especially with regard to writing for the school newspaper, literary review, and yearbook. He didn't follow a curriculum that led to a degree, focusing instead on the subjects that interested him the most—literature, rhetoric, and history. These were times of discovery and questioning for Sandburg. In *Ever the Winds of Chance,* he writes, "I was sure there are ten men in me and I do not know or understand one of them." He continues that:

> I had wonderings and hopes but they were vague and foggy. I couldn't see myself filling some definite niche in what is called a career. I might become a newspaper reporter, a foreign correspondent, and author of books, and advertising copywriter— or an actor, a Lyceum lecturer, an agitator, an orator—maybe a Congressman, or an independent drifter defiant of all respectable conformists. This was all misty.[11]

At Lombard College, Sandburg developed an exceptionally close and influential relationship with Professor Philip Green Wright. He called Wright—along with his wife, Paula, and her brother, the world-famous photographer, Edward Steichen—the three greatest influences of his life. Wright was an economist, a poet, a biographer, a mathematics and English instructor, an astronomer, a printer/publisher, and an activist for social justice. He formed the Poor Writers Club, giving a few students a forum to recite and critique their writings and discuss their developing ideals. He introduced Sandburg to Abraham Lincoln, Thomas Carlyle, William Shakespeare, Rudyard Kipling, Walt Whitman, John Ruskin, and in particular, Ralph Waldo Emerson.

In *The America of Carl Sandburg*, Professor Hazel Durnell writes:

> Sandburg's adherence to the idea of a national literature, interpretation of the commonplace in American life, and his conception of the poet's vital role in a changing society stem directly from the New England literary movement at the head of which was Emerson.[12]

Durnell goes on to say that the "Emersonian call for themes embracing the real life of the American citizen is carried out more voluminously in Sandburg's poetry than in that of any other American poet, dead or living."[13]

Sandburg continued to seek answers about his future direction in life after college. While traveling in the Midwest and East to sell pictures to view on a stereoscope, he worked just long enough to pay for his room and board, allowing ample time for reading, writing, and thinking. He shared his thoughts with his sister Mary, writing in 1903:

> What mood is this to-night, when I ask you to look not only on the good, but on the badness of Me. It's trust, if you know. But it's mighty hard when living a life packed with variety, to take up a

pen and make it walk around on the paper and tell you what's what.[14]

He also kept in close contact with Professor Wright, sharing his thoughts in letters and sending back samples of his writing. In his basement press, Wright published and printed three booklets by Sandburg: *In Reckless Ecstasy*, *Incidentals*, and *The Plaint of a Rose*. In *Incidentals*, Sandburg writes:

> Look at it in any line of work you please, in art, religion, business, or any other place of human effort. It is by getting away from known shores and sailing toward undiscovered countries and across uncharted seas, that men find new things that mean power or honor or love.[15]

The foundational years Sandburg chronicles in *Always the Young Strangers* and *Ever the Winds of Chance* point to the eclectic life of his adulthood. In *Carl Sandburg: A Study in Personality and Background*, author Karl Detzer concludes:

> By the time Sandburg was through with college in 1902, all the seeds of his later years were planted; the design of what he has become and what in the future he still will become was sketched in lightly, perhaps even a little grotesquely. His prairie boyhood, his hobo adventures, his early poverty, his love of the chase spurred on in the game he made of selling pictures, his affection for words, his interest in Lincoln, his sympathy for the underdog, his nonconformist way of life, the calluses on his hands—all these adding up to the Sandburg we know today.[16]

Chapter Two

Becoming the
Poet of the People

Sandburg's youth paralleled the nation's transition from an economy based on agriculture and small market towns to one centered on massive industrial development and urban growth fueled by advances in technology. Immigrants from Europe supplied much of the required labor, working long hours in often dangerous conditions for little pay. Business monopolies operated with little or no regulation, and Congress and the courts intervened when labor tried to organize.

This time was defined as the Progressive Era in American life and politics. Progressive reforms took many forms such as the good government movement, efforts to pass prohibition legislation, and government actions to bust corporate trusts. Other initiatives were pursued by American Socialism, which championed the growth of unions and the causes of the labor class (e.g., a minimum wage, the prohibition of child labor, workman's compensation, and industrial safety).

Sandburg joined the Social-Democratic Party of Wisconsin in the early 1900s. He organized rallies and wrote tracts and articles for the party, and in his widely distributed piece, "You and Your Job," he indicts the capitalistic system of his day:

> I believe in obstacles, but I say that a system such as the capitalist system, putting such obstacles as starvation, underfeeding, overwork, bad housing and perpetual uncertainty of work in the lives of human beings, is a pitiless, ignorant, blind, reckless, cruel mockery of a system.[17]

In a speech delivered in 1910, "A Labor Day Talk," Sandburg focused on the core economic problems of the working class and made a clarion call for action:

> Prosperity, luxury and magnificence for the few and death, hell, disease, misery and degradation for the many.
> Years ago we asked for old age pensions . . .
> But the years went by, we were laughed at as agitators, and it is today as it always was—old age is a time of life to be feared.
> Years ago we asked for a minimum wage to apply among all workers . . .
> But the years went by, we were ridiculed as impractical, and today millions of wage earners get pay so miserably low that they cannot live decently, cleanly, rightly . . .
> We have learned that Labor will have to fight its own battles. From now on we trust OURSELVES. . . .[18]

Organizers for the American Federation of Labor started reading a Sandburg poem at nearly every meeting, and union activists at the cotton mills of Gastonia, North Carolina, reprinted Sandburg's "Mill-Doors," on the back of the member application cards:

> YOU never come back.
> I say good-by when I see you going in the doors,
> The hopeless open doors that call and wait
> And take you then for—how many cents a day?
> How many cents for the sleepy eyes and fingers?
>
> I say good-by because I know they tap your wrists,
> In the dark, in the silence, day by day,
> And all the blood of you drop by drop,
> And you are old before you are young.
> You never come back.[19]

Poet of the People

In a 1908 letter to Sandburg, his soon-to-be wife, Lilian "Paula" Steichen, writes:

> Do tell me how you contrive to be a moral philosopher and a political agitator at one and the same time—and especially how you contrive to write such Poets' English one minute and the plain vernacular the next. The combination is baffling! Artist, poet-prophet, on the one hand; man of action, on the other.[20]

Sandburg continued to focus on labor issues in his reporting and poetry after moving to Chicago in 1912. He described the struggles and dreams of working-class people as well as their strength and determination to overcome hardships and oppression. In his highly acclaimed 1914 breakout poem, "Chicago," he speaks of the "faces of women and children . . . the marks of wanton hunger." And challenges readers to:

> Come and show me another city with lifted head singing so proud to be alive and coarse and strong and cunning . . .
> Proud to be Hog Butcher, Tool Maker, Stacker of Wheat, Player with Railroads and Freight Handler to the Nation.[21]

Chicago Poems, published in 1916, makes poetry out of the industrial city: its crowds of nameless faces, its buildings and transportation systems, its industries and labor conflicts, and its poverty and crime. In his book, *Carl Sandburg*, biographer and journalist Harry Golden writes, "It is not exaggerated to say you would learn more about the industrialization of America reading Sandburg's poems than you would learn about Elizabethan England reading Shakespeare's plays."[22] In *The America of Carl Sandburg*, Professor Hazel Durnell uses Sandburg's words to present a portrait of the people depicted in Sandburg's working-class poetry:

> From out of the great stormy maelstrom of its teeming masses, he drew for us the factory girl, the stockyard workers, the cabaret dancers, the weary toiler on his way to work, the shovelman in faded overalls, spattered with clay, the teamster, the negro dance with the lazy love banjo thrum, the sweating ditch-diggers, the railroad section hand, the stockyard worker's family, the expectant mothers, the

onion picker, who comes down Peoria Street with kindling wood on the top of her head; the crippled man ill with tuberculosis, Anna Imroth who lost her life in a factory fire, the green and gray streams of workin' girls moving in the early morning on the downtown streets; Mamie, who tired of the small town, came to Chicago hoping to find romance and real dreams "that neer go smash"; the hoboes of cattle cars; the gipsy woman and others.[23]

Sandburg understood the working class as critical to America's role as a leading industrial nation. He held that their life stories were a worthy subject for poetry— especially because they didn't always have the words or platform to speak for themselves. He believed "the laborer is not a machine, but that he has a soul and that his soul has a right to see and enjoy the clear sky, works of art, health, sanity, and beauty."[24] In particular, Sandburg's focus on the working class of the urban and rural Midwest was new to American literature. According to Durnell:

> Carl Sandburg's continuous effort to find a poetic outlet for the fast, hard, noisy, smoky, machine-ridden experience of Middle Western city people and for the dry, unshaded experience of Middle Western villagers and farmers has taken on the dimensions of a literary achievement, and one that no disparagement can minimize. In a generation in which most poets set themselves more manageable and more opportune tasks, he undertook to be the poet of a people among whom the sources of poetry, though by no means exhausted, were untapped, grown over and all but completely forgotten.[25]

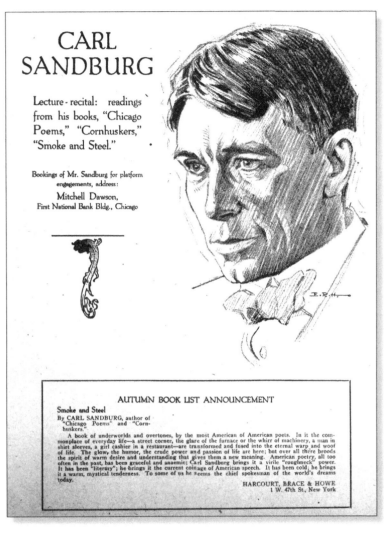

Leaflet advertising Carl Sandburg's lectures in 1920.

Sandburg employed their common speech and wrote in free verse, which was more readily understandable to workers than the allusion and traditional devices of rhymed poetry. Sandburg's use of slang in his writings shocked readers accustomed to finding elegance and grace in poetry. Some critics argued that what he wrote was not poetry at all. Paul Berman, the editor of *Carl Sandburg: Selected Poems*, describes Sandburg's work as "Poetry that doesn't bubble up from the mystic soul but precipitates instead from already-existing sounds and phrases."[26] In *Carl Sandburg*, author Richard Crowder notes:

> [Sandburg was] the first poet of modern times actually to use the language of the people as his almost total means of expression. . . . Sandburg had entered into the language of the people; he was not looking at it as a scientific phenomenon or a curiosity. . . . He was at home with it.[27]

Sandburg wrote from his own experience as a laborer in his early life and as a reporter covering labor, poverty, and crime. He said: "Here is the difference between Dante, Milton, and me. They wrote about hell and never saw the place. I wrote about Chicago after looking the town over for years and years."[28] Sandburg wrote about what he knew and felt deeply. American journalist Walter Yust commented that:

> Sandburg's poems are not an expression of eccentric individualism but are an honest attempt to express a richly developed personality. That is why they are authentic poems. That is why Sandburg must discard rhyme and conscious meter; that is why he must use living "common" words. Sandburg's poems are Sandburg. They are powerful, live, brutal, gentle, and humorous—and so is he.[29]

The People, Yes

The Great Depression in the 1930s led to mass unemployment and underemployment throughout the United States. The American landscape was spoiled with shuttered factories and businesses, house and farm foreclosures, and soup and bread lines. People began to think the new realities of their lives were permanent. Rather than holding a failed economic system accountable, they blamed themselves, creating a legacy of hopelessness. Sandburg's *The People, Yes* is a response to these times.

The People, Yes is an epic, book-long single poem organized in discrete categories (proverbs, anecdotes, yarns, cliches, biographies, legends, character sketches, folk-wisdom, dialogues, and songs) and thematic clusters (greed, class struggle, war, love, marriage, hope, materialism, and peace). At first glance, the work appears unstructured, even incoherent, but it "is in reality a carefully crafted modern epic poem, a pageant more than a narrative, a highly original fusion of unorthodox, seemingly disparate elements,"[30] concluded Sandburg biographer Penelope Niven.

In the foreword to *The People, Yes*, Sandburg writes that the work:

> Being several stories and psalms nobody would
> want to laugh at
> interspersed with memoranda variations worth a
> second look
> along with sayings and yarns traveling on grief
> and
> laughter
> running sometimes as a fugitive air in the classic

manner
breaking into jig time and tap dancing nohow
classical
and further broken by plan and irregular sounds
and echoes form
the roar and whirl of street crowds, work gangs,
sidewalk clamor,
with interludes of midnight cool blue and
inviolable
stars
over the phantom frames of skyscrapers.[31]

In *The People, Yes,* Sandburg acknowledges the hardships that were so pervasive during the Great Depression. The unemployed were:

Without a stake in the country
Without jobs or nest eggs
Marching they don't know where
Marching north south west—[32]

Families struggled with:

Payments on the car, and bungalow, the radio, the
electric icebox, accumulated interest on loans
for past payments, the writhing point of
where the money will come from . . .[33]

And everyone felt the uncertainty of the times.

And in the air a decree: life is a gamble; take a
chance; you pick a number and see what you
get: anything can happen in this sweepstakes:

around the corner may be prosperity or the
worst depression yet: who knows?
Nobody. . . .[34]

Sandburg's *The People, Yes* also affirmed the American
people's gifts for survival. He wrote that:

The people will live on
The learning and blundering people will live on.
They will be tricked and sold and again sold
And go back to the nourishing earth for
rootholds,
The people so peculiar in renewal and
comeback,
You can't laugh off their capacity to take it.[35]

He concludes his epic poem with a recapitulation of
images, themes, proverbs, and aphorisms, which are juxta-
posed with the poet's perennial unanswerable question:

The old anvil laughs at many broken hammers.
there are men who can't be bought.
the fireborn are at home in fire.
the stars make no noise.
you can't hinder the wind from blowing.
time is a great teacher.
who can live without hope?
In the darkness with a great bundle of grief
the people march,
In the night, and overhead a shovel of stars for
keeps, the people march:
"Where to? what next?"[36]

Sandburg continued to actively pursue his life's work during his final twenty-two years on his Flat Rock, North Carolina, farm, writing one-third of his publications there. He was eight-five years old when his last collection of poems, *Honey and Salt*, was published. He said, "The brightest, most lasting happiness I know is that which comes from yearning, striving, struggling, fashioning, this way and that, till a thing is done."[37] Although Sandburg achieved great fame, he never abandoned his common, working-class roots. In his works and in his personal life, he remained true to his reputation as the poet of the people.

———

Chapter Three

Three Acres and Liberty: Cultivation and Husbandry by the Sandburg Women

When Sandburg was growing up in the 1880s and 1890s, horsepower meant traditional agricultural practice with horses, not tractors. Industrial agriculture was just beginning; America would not become a truly urban nation until the 1920s. In the poem "New Farm Tractor," Sandburg looks back on these earlier times and writes, "I crave a team of long ear mules on the steering wheel—it's good-by now to leather reins and the songs of the old mule skinners."[38]

But in the youths of both Carl and Paula, growing vegetables and raising animals at home was a common aspiration if not a reality. People believed that a farmer could live off what he raised and, unlike most working-class people, the farmer couldn't be fired, laid off, or have a salary reduced. The Sandburg family dreamed of leaving the railroad town of Galesburg and moving to farmland they had bought on the prairie. When the Panic of 1893 saw the family income drastically cut, their hopes were dashed. To make ends meet, the Sandburgs ate bread spread with lard, and Carl dropped out of school to work. He never forgot about being poor.

The Steichen family (Paula's parents) eventually settled on rural land outside Milwaukee, where Paula's father kept chickens and grew vegetables on several acres. When Carl and Paula lived in Wisconsin during the early days of their marriage, it was clear that Paula had inherited her father's passion for growing crops and raising farm animals. She yearned to save enough money for farmland, feeling cooped up in rented housing, which the newlyweds named "The Rooms." Helga, the Sandburg's youngest daughter, recalls:

> [My mother] had read a book called *Three Acres & Liberty* and she told my father, "I spent yesterday evening 7–9 at the library reading this book—all about hoeing, and ploughing, and weeding, and guano, and plaster etc., etc.! Wonderful! . . . I am in favor of planning things somehow—someway— . . . so we'll get some simoleons— . . . The more I read, the more I realize the advantage of a little capital for current expenses—fertilizers, tools, trees & bush-fruit to set out, strawberry plants etc., etc. . . .
>
> If you can get any pointers from Pa how (not) to manage our chicken farm—so as to have our eggs cost us 5 cents apiece (net)—why get the Pointers! Go ahead! . . . I've a lot of literature on Poultry . . . and they make exciting reading![39]

True to the plan—and guided by her University of Chicago genetics classes—Paula used an incubator to bring 300 chicks to broiler size. She spent sleepless nights tending to the eggs. About one-half would not hatch or died before maturity, including chicks that escaped the chicken yard and were run over by a streetcar.

In 1914, the Sandburgs purchased their first home in the Chicago suburb of Maywood. While serving as an overseas correspondent in Sweden during World War I, Sandburg wrote that "this will be a wonderful spring—when we can start growing things in our own soil!"[40] Their backyard saw a cherry tree yield fruit for pies and jellies, and a vegetable garden dug. Paula declared, "We must surely get a wheelbarrow now! And start an asparagus bed and strawberry plants!"[41]

After a few years, the family moved to nearby Elmhurst. Their new home, a former farmhouse built in 1857, already had a garden, and they bought the lot next door. In their new home—which the Sandburgs called "Happiness House"—they "enjoyed the isolation granted by unpaved roads, privacy insured by trees, and rustic beauty of pastures stretching behind the house,"[42] noted biographer Harry Golden.

In 1927, following the financial success of *Abraham Lincoln: The Prairie Years*, the Sandburgs built a lakefront home in Harbert, Michigan. They christened their five acres the Paw-Paw Patch after the trees that grew there. Soon an adjacent piece of land was bought to expand their space for gardening. Helga explains that her mother ". . . is going to dig up the sand and order a truckload of manure and fence in the place and make a garden proper."[43] Trees were planted for protection against sand blown from the dunes along Lake Michigan. Packets of seed were bought, and rows were laid out with stakes and string. An orchard with apples, peaches, apricots, plums, cherries, and nectarines was started. As a Depression-era housewife, Paula was proud that the family grew so much of the food they needed.

The Paw-Paw Patch was alive with animals as well, including six gray Toulouse geese, a few white Pekin ducks, and a flock of twenty-five White Rock pullets. There were rabbits and chickens for food, and Helga wrote that she and her mother "became proficient at the swift kill and the skinning, plucking and eviscerating of whatever was for our table."[44] The girls kept guinea pigs, mice, and white rats housed in various pens and cages about the cellar and garage. Helga adopted a mongoose she called Davy. Helga noted that she "prowls through the jungle with Davy, his rat coat sleek, his long pink tail hanging down, his whiskers resting on her neck. He is a mongoose—Rikki-Tikki-Tavi in Kipling's *The Jungle Book*, and has just killed the cobra, Nag."[45]

Sandburg's discussion of goat raising in his 1920 newsreel review, "Ain't Nature Wonderful in New Science Films," foreshadowed goats in the family a decade later. But it was an adolescent's plea for a Jersey cow that launched the family's love affair with goats. Helga wrote that she wanted "her hands on the warm smooth soft hair of a huge creature . . . to feel the rubbery nose, to smell the sweet breath, to hear the low voice."[46] Carl countered that a cow was too big for a girl to handle and too expensive to keep. He suggested a goat as a substitute.

The Sandburgs bought enough goats for a small herd they named Chikaming, after a local Michigan tribe of Native Americans. Paula began to breed her does, taking two of them to a big white-horned buck, which Carl described as "affirmative in his attitude toward life."[47] The Sandburgs built a large barn that Carl called "the most colossal barn in the great state of Michigan . . . a regular Old Testament edifice, which would hold more goats, kids and revolutionary pamphlets than any other barn in Michigan."[48]

In 1935, Carl described the evolving and integrated nature of the farm, which often expanded when he was away traveling:

> [I]n February, they decided a goat herd, hens, ducks, geese and rabbits were not enough, and took on a horse. When I left in April for ten days, they took on two pigs. The horse can live on what the goats reject. And the pigs get by on leavings no others will touch, though like very ancient farmers we cannot begin to get God's intention in curling the tails of the pigs.[49]

Horses became part of the Sandburgs' life in Michigan and would continue to be for more than forty years. One mare called Silver had the build of a circus horse and could, on command, kneel to lie down or rear spectacularly. She took Helga soaring over the dunes, which prompted her to write: "There goes Brunhilda, as she gallops by, braids flying."[50] And, in a more practical role, Silver plowed the garden.

The Sandburgs called the summer of 1935 the season of the three Gs—garden, geese, and goats. The Sandburgs got all the milk they needed from their goats and bought a separator to make cheese and butter. They canned and stored what they could. To help with the farm work—and protest the injustice of the Japanese-American internment camps—the Sandburgs arranged for the release of Miss Suano Imoto by guaranteeing her employment.

Old newspaper friends from Chicago occasionally visited the Sandburg's Paw-Paw Patch. They mischievously printed a business card for Sandburg, not wanting him to be embarrassed when travelers he met on trains asked what he did for a living. Sandburg carried the card in his wallet.

> ## NORTH AMERICAN
> *Association of Paw-Paw Growers*
>
> ## CARL SANDBURG
> *Chairman of the Board of Directors*

A desire to expand their goat herd led the Sandburg family in 1945 to buy the Connemara Farm in Flat Rock, North Carolina. The farm's 245 acres included ample spring pasture for their goats, which provided them exercise and choice of roughage and grasses—something not possible on the much smaller Michigan property. Connemara came with several barns and other farm structures to which a milking parlor in the barn and a separate milk house building were added.

Paula continued her practice of carefully recording the type and amount of feed, breeding decisions, and resulting births. Cabinets that held thousands of breeding records can still be seen in the farm office in the Connemara home. The Sandburgs showed Saanen, Toggenburg, and Nubian breeds throughout the South, winning top awards in all categories. Goat's milk was purchased by several regional dairies. Paula published articles in goat journals and made speeches at conferences and agricultural schools—talking with folks who often as not had never heard of Carl Sandburg. She also helped establish the American Dairy Goat Association and served as its director for over ten years. In 1960, a Toggenburg named Jennifer II was recognized as the top producing doe in the world. Weighing 170 pounds, she produced more than two gallons of milk per day—her weight in milk almost every week.

A caretaker and his family and temporary workers shared in the immense labor needed for a farm this size as did all the Sandburg daughters. Eldest daughter, Margaret, cared for a wild, overgrown, fenced garden of roses, peonies, and perennials. Middle daughter, Janet, quiet and shy around people, thrived in her role of feeding several groups of young goats two to three times each day. Helga worked daily at the barn and, for a while, ran the goat operations with her second husband.

Other farm animals joined the goats at Connemara. Pastures became dotted with flocks of sheep and a few massive Black Angus cows, and nearby, a pen of hogs was set. Several farm buildings housed varieties of chickens, and a flock of ducks lived in the pasture pond. There were as many as ten horses, which were used for pleasure as well as for plowing fields or clearing snow. Helga's beehives maintained a steady flow of honey for the family, especially for Carl's coffee. The Sandburg grandchildren, John and Paula, kept hutches of rabbits and guinea pigs. For a time, Helga raised registered Siamese cats and Doberman Pinschers.

The plant kingdom was not neglected on the farm. Flowers and vegetables were started in two greenhouses— one attached to the side of the house and the other next to the main garden. Strawberries were set in beds, and apple trees were pruned in the orchard. Fruits and vegetables were canned and frozen, cheeses were made from goat's milk, and meats from the farm were prepared in the kitchen.

Motivated by economic necessity, scientific curiosity, or the desire for a simple, natural life, the Sandburgs' adventures in cultivation and husbandry brought them great joy wherever they lived. Youngest daughter, Helga, beautifully captures these sentiments in the poem "some proclamations to an old stump," where she writes "me for Thoreau and the nine bean rows / me for the simple life / me for springs-kids nuzzling my fingers . . ."[51]

Chapter Four

Muckraking Reporter and Columnist

Sandburg delivered newspapers as a schoolboy in Galesburg and later as a teenager read newspapers between stops delivering milk. He especially enjoyed the big city presses. During his first trip to Chicago, he walked by the *Chicago Daily News* and the *Chicago Tribune* buildings. He left without a suitcase—just his father's railroad pass and one dollar and fifty cents for the three-day excursion.

Sandburg first wrote news stories during the Spanish-American War in 1898 when he served with Company C, Sixth Infantry Regiment of Illinois Volunteers. He described how he and his fellow soldiers experienced the conflict in stories posted to the *Galesburg Evening Mail*. As a veteran, Sandburg was awarded a one-year scholarship to Lombard College where he gained invaluable experience as he wrote, formatted, and edited the newspaper and yearbook.

For a short time after college, Sandburg wrote a column for the *Galesburg Evening Mail*, hoping it would be discovered by a big-city editor. He named it "Inklings and Idlings." He left Galesburg for Chicago in 1905, never to return as a full-time resident. He then worked for a variety of newspapers: *Unity,* a magazine of the Unitarian Church;

To-Morrow, which provided room and board, but no salary; the *Lyceumite*, a periodical for platform artists; the *Day Book*, which accepted no advertising and had a strong social justice message; and *System: The Magazine of Business*.

Sandburg's left-leaning politics attracted a recruiter who was looking for someone to organize the growing Social-Democratic Party in the Southern Wisconsin territory. He accepted the offer and moved to Wisconsin in 1907, where he gave stump speeches and wrote articles and pamphlets for the party and wrote editorials for the *International Socialist Review*—which also published a few of his early poems.

Sandburg next accepted the position of secretary for the socialist mayor of Milwaukee—similar to chief of staff today. He also wrote stories for a variety of publications: the *Milwaukee Journal*, the *Milwaukee Daily News*, and the *Milwaukee Sentinel*. And he penned a light column called "Zig-Zags." After the defeat of the Social-Democratic Party in Milwaukee, he moved back to Chicago. The city was known for its muckraker reporters, such as Ida M. Tarbell (*History of the Standard Oil Company*) and Upton Sinclair (*The Jungle*).

He worked short-term for several publications, including a few weeks with a Hearst publication that he left after being pressured to slant his writing toward conservative interests. He then accepted a position at the *Chicago Daily News* at half the salary; he remained there for twelve years. In 1927, Sandburg turned down another offer by a Hearst paper, this time for the huge sum of $75,000 for two years of editorial writing. Sandburg explained that "the higher I got in figures, the more sure I was that we couldn't agree on a high enough figure till I get three or four books done that must get written."[52]

Young Carl Sandburg at a typewriter, possibly at the *Chicago Daily News*.
Used with permission of the Rare Book & Manuscript Library,
University of Illinois, Urbana-Champaign

For the *Chicago Daily News*, he wrote news stories and editorials about social and economic issues: child labor, working conditions, labor strikes, income inequality, women's rights, crime, migration and immigration, and urban industrial growth. Despite his own political inclinations, he was scrupulously fair and objective in his writings. Fellow reporter Harry Hansen describes Sandburg's keen sense of social awareness as well as his humor:

The warmth that Carl had for people was something that you never forgot. He was from the beginning a newspaperman and he had the qualities of a newspaperman. He had awareness. A newspaperman somehow knows what is going on around him. He doesn't live in isolation. Carl had a keen sense of justice. He hated injustice and it runs all through his career, runs in his poems. Carl also had a great sense of proportion. He enjoyed humor. He found all sort of amusing things in clippings and his pockets were always full of clippings in those days at the *Chicago Daily News* and at any time, he would take one out and read it and expect you to chuckle just as much as he did.[53]

After a long day writing news stories, Sandburg labored late in the night on his poetry—often writing about the same events, people, and issues he covered for the press. His poetic style was also influenced by the concise and direct style of news reporting. The following examples are all found in Sandburg's first book of poems, *Chicago Poems*:

"They Will Say"

You took little children away from the sun and the dew, . . .
To eat dust in their throats and die empty-hearted,
for a little handful of pay on a few Saturday nights.[54]

"Anna Imroth"

But all of the others got down and they are safe and this is the only
One of the factory girls who wasn't lucky in making the jump
When the fire broke.[55]

"Ice Handler"

He remembers when the union was organized, he broke the noses of two scabs and loosened the nuts so the wheels came off six different wagons one morning, and he came around and watched the ice melt in the street.[56]

"Child of the Romans"

The dago shovelman sits by the railroad track
Eating a noon meal of bread and bologna
A train whirls by, and men and women at tables
Alive with red roses and yellow jonquils,
Eat steaks, running with brown gravy,
Strawberries and cream, eclairs and coffee.[57]

"Skyscraper"

By day the skyscraper looms in the smoke and sun and
    has a soul.
By night the skyscraper looms in the smoke and the stars
    and has a soul.[58]

World War I and the Chicago Race Riots

Sandburg initially saw World War I as an exploitation of the working class by wealthy elites and opposed the war. But once the United States was engaged, he was fully on board. He did continue to rail, however, against severe and unjust government censorship. The jailing of long-time friend and presidential candidate, Eugene Debs, was particularly galling to him. In Sweden for five months during the end of the war, Sandburg wrote dispatches as a correspondent for the Newspaper Enterprise Association—the forerunner of the Associated Press. Both his departure to and return from Europe was delayed by the State Department due to his earlier association with American socialism and his continued interest in the laboring classes. It also didn't help that his name was sometimes confused with the known communist, Karl Sandberg.

Sandburg returned to the *Chicago Daily News* at the end of the war. He covered the impact of Black migration from the rural South to the industrialized North, which was driven by the workforce needs of the war as well as a desire of Blacks to escape the Jim Crow South. Even though African Americans had served honorably in the war, returning Black soldiers found race relations hadn't changed much back home. The Ku Klux Klan was in ascendancy and widespread lynching was a national disgrace. The competition between returning white and African American soldiers for jobs and homes led to violent riots all over the country.

The Chicago Race Riots in 1919 were among the worst. They were sparked by the drowning of a young African American man at the hands of whites after he accidentally drifted onto the white side of the beach. In total, 38 persons died, 537 were injured, and 1,000 were left homeless. Blacks suffered the most.

With an understanding of racial issues far ahead of his time, Sandburg pushed back on the prevailing belief that Blacks were largely responsible for the riots. In his writing, he explored the discrimination in housing, politics, and organized labor that fueled social divides. He analyzed government statistics and conducted first-person interviews to learn what had happened and why. He spent days roaming Chicago's Black neighborhoods interviewing shopkeepers, housewives, factory workers, preachers, gamblers, and pimps. He called for federal reform policy and aid, lobbying for a level playing field for Blacks. He wrote:

> The truth is there ain't no negro problem any more than there's an Irish problem or a Russian or a Polish or a Jewish or any other problem. There is only the human problem. All we demand is the open door. You give us that, and we won't ask nothin' more of you.[59]

The series of articles about the riots were compiled into Sandburg's first book of prose, *The Chicago Race Riots*. The Chicago Commission on Race Relations issued a commendation saying that the publication was "well-received and gave a necessary balance, not the more usual publication of stories involving Negroes in crimes."[60] Sandburg's writings investigated the underlying causes of the race riot and suggested policy to address it. Biographer and fellow journalist Harry Golden writes that Sandburg's "concern with the Negroes' drive for equality and justice has affected every part of him, politically and artistically. . . . The problem of racial equality has never been far from Sandburg's mind."[61]

Sandburg uses lynching as the metaphor for the race riots in the poem "Man, The Man-Hunter."

> I SAW Man, the man-hunter, Hunting with a
> torch in one hand
> And a kerosene can in the other,
> Hunting with guns, ropes, shackles.
>> I listened
>> And the high cry rang,

The high cry of Man, the man-hunter:
We'll get you yet, you sbxyzch!*
   I listened later.
   The high cry rang:
Kill him! Kill him! The sbxyzch!
In the morning the sun saw
Two butts of something, a smoking rump,
And a warning in charred wood:
                Well, we got him,
                The   sbxyzch.[62]

Sbxyzah: son of a bitch in oral Chicago slang

In 1965 at the height of the modern Civil Rights Movement, Sandburg received the NAACP Lifetime Membership Award as a prophet of civil rights in our time. The first white person to receive the honor, he prominently displayed the commemorative plaque in the downstairs study at Connemara. His Pulitzer Prizes, literary medals, and dozens of honorary doctorates were stored out of sight.

World War II and the *Home Front Memo*

In addition to writing columns for newspapers and magazines during World War II, Sandburg penned poems and gave public speeches at rallies and on the radio. These were compiled into a book titled *Home Front Memo*. The book's selections extensively referenced historical, literary, and contemporary sources—American presidents and politicians, scientists and inventors, labor leaders, classic and contemporary authors, sports figures, and celebrities. Stories were replete with folk wisdom, anecdotes, and parables, most

often focusing on the common soldier and common working people. He wrote that:

> The common man is the main figure in the fight-
> ing and the production. The forces working for
> him are immense. There are movements and ideas
> having voices—and power. The saying "It is a peo-
> ple's war" is not empty.[63]

Sandburg presented all sides of controversial issues but
took strong stands when he believed it was needed. In particular, he worried that the free press could be misused by
a minority to the point where voluntary censorship might
become compulsory. He felt that the "press must be vigilant to
defend the right of criticism everywhere in order that it may
be curtailed nowhere."[64] He also points to the dangers of:

> The hate-ridden who make a domestic business of
> their hate and peddle it for political and journalis-
> tic profit, the fear-bitten whose personal necessity
> seems to dictate that they should infect others with
> fear and foreboding.[65]

He pondered what a just peace at war's end would look
like. Will the ending of World War II be followed by the
same kind of useless feeling so many people in America had
at the end of World War I? Will Black soldiers be able to live
with white soldiers on terms of honest, objective equality?

> We in the United States of America are going to
> make decisions, for instance, as to whether the
> Negro soldier who has borne hardships and wounds

in the services of his country shall be stopped from voting as a freeman and a citizen on the ground that he has not paid a poll tax now required from him in various Southern states. We are going to make decisions whether it is possible and practicable or pen new lines of office, factory, shop, and mill jobs to Negroes in recognition of service and sacrifice they gave to the war.[66]

In admiration of Sandburg's wartime coverage, U.S. Navy Fleet Admiral Chester W. Nimitz gave him a photograph of the Japanese surrender at Tokyo Bay in September 1945. The inscription on the photograph stated: "To Carl Sandburg—with best wishes, great respect and admiration. C.W. Nimitz, Fleet Admiral, U.S. Navy."[67]

Sandburg moved to Connemara in his sixties. He stayed abreast of world affairs by subscribing to more than fifty newspapers and magazines—none of which he seemed to throw away—and watching nightly newscasts. Sandburg continued to write articles, editorials, and columns, and his perspectives on issues were highly valued and often syndicated in newspapers and magazines that reached throughout the country. Even *Playboy Magazine* published six poems and a parable. Sandburg remarked, "It was fun to be read by the most gustatory audience of readers in America, all of them definitely opposed to artificial insemination."[68] In 1960, when Sandburg was in his eighties, the news industry came to Connemara to film an episode of Edward R. Murrow's television program, *See It Now*. The circle was completed. Sandburg, the newspaper man, had become the news.

Chapter Five

Speaking Across America

In the early nineteenth century, the lyceum and Chautauqua movements brought oration to audiences beyond the university classroom. Founded in 1826, the lyceum continued the practice of the ancient Greece gymnasium where debates and lectures on topics of current interest took place. Among lyceum's well-known speakers were Ralph Waldo Emerson, Frederick Douglass, Daniel Webster, and Susan B. Anthony. The Chautauqua movement began at a New York Christian retreat center in 1874. It quickly expanded into a national institution—especially in rural and small-town America, which had become more accessible by an expanding railroad system. Mark Twain, Theodore Roosevelt, Booker T. Washington, and Clarence Darrow were among the circuit's leading lecturers.

In the mid- to late-nineteenth century, public oratory became the greatest show in town, and it provided the foundation for twentieth-century performance on radio, television, and the cinema. People gathered in the hundreds and thousands to attentively listen—sometimes for several hours—to talks delivered in grange halls, civic auditoriums, college lecture rooms, and church sanctuaries. It was a powerful source of education, edification, and entertainment.

The array of talks on science, health, religion, philosophy, literature, and politics seemed endless.

In *Always the Young Strangers*, Sandburg recalls hearing lecturers who stopped in Galesburg on their way west: the populist William Jennings Bryan promoted his candidacy during a rail stop tour, and the photographer Jacob Riis described the poverty of immigrants in New York City tenements.

For a brief time after college, Sandburg promoted the speaking industry by writing thumbnail biographies in the speaker's magazine, the *Lyceumite*, and helped schedule and promote performances in his role as associate editor. Eventually, Sandburg joined the ranks of the most sought-after orators of his time.

Sandburg gave his first speech in elementary school when he competed in the Demorest Silver Medal Declamation contest. The national competition provided a book of speeches about the evils of alcohol. He memorized the shortest speech but froze when it came time to give it. The medal went to his sister Mary, and Carl vowed he would not let a speech get away from him again.

As a Lombard College student, Sandburg joined the debate and literary club, completed six courses in elocution, and took many classes in history and literature—which provided content for his later lectures. For his presentation, "A Man with Ideals," he won the coveted college Swan Award. In a harbinger of his later focus, he defended John Ruskin's thesis that "the laborer is not a machine, but that he has a soul and that his soul has a right to see and enjoy the clear sky, works of art, health, sanity and beauty."[69] He came to keenly appreciate that delivering content via the spoken word is fundamentally different from providing content as written word. He saw how audiences could be moved by powerful oration delivered with passion by a speaker who honestly believed in what he or she was saying.

During his few years as a political organizer in Southern Wisconsin, Sandburg earned most of his meager income by giving soap box speeches and passing the hat. Eugene Debs, the presidential candidate for the Socialist Party, saw Sandburg as "one of the most brilliant young orators in the Socialist movement in the United States,"[70] and said, "No one who has heard Sandburg has failed to be impressed by the dignity of his presence, the force of his logic, the eloquence of his speech, and the sincerity of his purpose."[71]

The Swedish spoken and sung by his immigrant parents helped shape the pitch and pace of Sandburg's voice. And as an adult, he worked hard to develop his unique style of oratory. He practiced speeches to rows of cornstalks and acres of cabbage heads when traveling from one small prairie town to another selling stereoscopes. He studied the oratory styles and subject matters of other lecturers, and noted how audiences responded. He worked and reworked his own speeches and practiced these on diverse audiences: members of a Black literary club, inmates at a prison, and a congregation of a Universal Unitarian Church. He received encouragement and constructive criticism to a speech delivered at the renowned Elbert Hubbard Roycroft Center in New York. When complimented on his voice years later, he replied, "I worked hard to make it like that—no one knows how hard."[72]

In 1900, on the back page of his early work, *Incidentals*, Sandburg listed the titles of three lectures he was prepared to deliver. By 1904, he saw lecturing as a promising way of making money, and by 1908, he was delivering lectures in Michigan, Wisconsin, Illinois, and Pennsylvania. His rich, strong baritone voice was used with dramatic effect to captivate his audiences. Biographer Penelope Niven notes that:

> It was no simple feat to engage a crowd for nearly two hours, enthrall them with words so they stood without a bit of noise throughout the entire address . . . to deliver stock speeches with the fresh, seamlessly spontaneous passion of the consummate actor.[73]

Eventually Sandburg included his own poetry and later folk songs with his lectures. North Callahan in *Carl Sandburg: Lincoln of Our Literature* notes, "he sang out his rhythmic word pictures until his audiences were fascinated by the sounds alone—which is just what he meant for them to be."[74]

Sandburg believed that a writer had an obligation to speak to current events. He gave hundreds of speeches during his life; many focused on the issues he strongly believed in such as American democracy and social justice for the working class. This held true for the platform speeches he first developed and for speeches he later gave at larger venues and on the radio.

Platform and Political Speeches

On Memorial Day 1904, Sandburg made a pilgrimage to the resting place of Walt Whitman and laid a rose on his tomb. Sandburg developed the lecture, "An American Vagabond or Poet of Democracy," which painted Whitman as seeker, dreamer, vagabond, and social activist. He reworked this theme in several lectures.

In "The Three Blunders of Civilization: War, Child Labor, and the Death Penalty," Sandburg awakened audiences to the horror and brutally of these "blunders of civilization." Here, and in the lecture "Making a New Civilization," he explored the promise of socialism in America. He left the Democratic-Socialist Party during World War I, and he never joined another political party, but he did actively support liberal policies and Democratic candidates and officeholders. (On a few occasions, Sandburg was considered as a possible candidate for both houses of Congress, but he never pursued those opportunities.) That said, Sandburg's socialist ideology continued to surface in his political writings and speeches throughout his career.

Sandburg's *Home Front Memo* contains several of the most important political speeches he delivered during the World War II era: everything from home front issues of scarcity and race relations to battlefield outcomes and fascist atrocities. The work includes seven platform speeches and radio broadcasts as well as essays, poems, and newspaper columns.

In 1940, he delivered an election-eve broadcast during the last five minutes of a two-hour nationwide radio program. His job was to convince independent voters, like him, to support President Franklin Delano Roosevelt in his bid for an unprecedented third term in office. He compared FDR to Lincoln, quoting a letter written during Lincoln's reelection campaign: "And although he does not do everything that you and I would like, the question recurs, whether we can elect a man who would. If he is not the best conceivable President, he is the best possible."[75] Sandburg received a letter from FDR praising Sandburg's political acumen:

> You are such an understanding soul. And can make allowances with fairness for the weaknesses and frailties of human nature. You are one of the few people who can truly understand the perplexities, the complications, the failures and the successes of what goes on in Washington.[76]

Sandburg also worked for the Kennedy election in 1960. After the election, he wrote the foreword for a book of Kennedy speeches entitled *To Turn the Tide*. First Lady Jacqueline Kennedy hosted an evening with Sandburg at the White House. President Johnson awarded him the Presidential Medal of Freedom in 1964.

In a speech at Madison Square Garden in 1941, Sandburg touched on several aspects of American exceptionalism: wide involvement in the democratic system and government from the bottom up, free speech and free thought, economic and social mobility and choice, and the ability of the system to stretch and change while maintaining core beliefs. He asks and answers why the American people support democracy:

> Because we have not yet seen a system that works better, because by the very nature of the workings of the democratic system in the long run it gives more people more chance to think, to speak, to

decide on their way of life to shape and change their way or life if they want to, than any other system. It has more give and take, more resilience, ductility, and malleability, more crazy foolishness and more grand wisdom, than any other system.[77]

He warns of individuals (both domestic and foreign) and forces (especially intolerance and misinformation and lies) that mitigate against the democratic system in America:

We know who and what we mean when we say there are those who soil the word "democracy" with lies. They are haters of political freedom for all men, scorners of religious freedom, race-haters, propagandists who believe they stand a chance of adding one hate movement to another till they have enough hates to discredit the democratic system so that the people will turn in desperation to something else, anything else.[78]

Sandburg's fame as a speaker grew throughout his lifetime. In 1929, when he was fifty-one years old, he delivered the Phi Beta Kappa lecture at Harvard and recited an original poem written for the occasion. After getting the nod from such a prestigious institution, he quipped, "Harvard has more of a reputation to lose than I have."[79]

In 1958, the inaugural year of the Grammy Awards, the music industry formally recognized Sandburg's achievement in spoken performance. He was nominated for "best performance documentary or spoken word." He won the following year for his reading of Aaron Copeland's *A Lincoln Portrait*, and he received another nomination in 1962 for readings of his poetry. He released seven vinyl records that featured his poetry or prose readings. These included poetry readings from *The People, Yes* and a collection of poems for children, and prose excerpts from his autobiography, books on Lincoln, and writings for children.

Sandburg's voice was heard throughout America for half a century. The quality of delivery and the authenticity of content gave his speeches their great appeal. President Lyndon B. Johnson observed that "Carl Sandburg was more than the voice of America, more than the poet of its strength and genius. He was America."[80]

Chapter Six

Teaching America Its Songs

Enjoyed throughout contemporary society, folk songs are respected as authentic revelations of the American experience that are handed down orally from generation to generation. During Sandburg's childhood and young adulthood, however, folk songs were thought to be crude, unworthy of public performance, literary criticism, or formal preservation. School-age children and adults typically sang sentimental songs about home and family, which included moral messages about patriotism, industry, cleanliness, and reverence for God—but not about commonplace experience.

Sandburg's interest in singing and playing music started in his youth. His father accompanied the one Swedish song he knew on an accordion and a little foot pedal organ, and Mary, Sandburg's sister, played popular songs on the family piano. Sandburg made a willow whistle—a comb with paper that sounded like a harmonica—and a cigar box banjo. He later bought a kazoo, a concertina, and a two-dollar banjo from a pawn shop. He paid a quarter for three banjo lessons. One of his friends taught him minstrel and popular songs and ballads, and he took a few lessons from a choirmaster. He sang in his college glee club and with a local barbershop quartet. Sometimes between dances at Lombard College, he strummed a guitar and sang popular ballads and folk songs.

Carl Sandburg playing the guitar at the University of South Carolina.

At the age of thirty-nine, Sandburg bought his first guitar—six years before his first book of poetry was published. It was an ornate parlor instrument sold by Sears & Roebuck. He wrote his wife, Paula, "I forgot to tell you that the S-S now have a guitar and there will be songs warbled and melodies whistled to the . . . thrumming of Paula-and-Cully's new stringed instrument."[81] The convention, "S-S," meant Sandburg-Steichen—a favorite term of endearment for the couple.

When Sandburg added folk songs to his lectures, he drew larger and larger audiences, saying, "If you don't care for them and want to leave the hall it will be all right with me. I'll only be doing what I'd be doing if I were at home, anyway."[82] They stayed, and for the rest of his long and prolific life, Sandburg sang on stages across the country. The moniker "the old troubadour" given to Sandburg by his friend, architect Frank Lloyd Wright, stuck.

A young Sandburg jotted down the lyrics of songs he collected: from friends and folks he met while working numerous jobs around Galesburg; from rivermen, steve-dores, farmhands, hoboes, cowboys, and railroad men he met during his travels as a hobo; and from town and farm families he encountered when canvassing as a door-to-door salesman. According to biographer Penelope Niven, "He was becoming a keen listener and observer, filing away the rhythms of a diverse language and the faces of the men who told him their stories, false or true."[83] As he sang and lectured throughout America, his musical collection grew. Literary colleagues, union organizers, college students and professors, and obscure nineteenth-century songbooks added songs to his collection.

With natural instincts as a performer, Sandburg genu-inely liked his audiences and his contact with them. There was a haunting quality to his voice, which he delivered with impeccable timing. Journalist and longtime friend Harry Golden shared that "I've heard him sing in a huge audi-torium in a whisper, and yet the entire audience sat silent, spellbound."[84] *Chicago Daily News* colleague Lloyd Lewis remarked that "Sandburg may not be a great singer, but his singing is great. He is the last of the troubadours; the last of the nomad artists who hunted out the songs people made up, and then sang them back to the people like a revela-tion."[85] Lewis continued:

For every song that he sings there comes a mood, a character, an emotion . . . you see farmhands wailing their lonely ballads, hill-billies lamenting over drowned girls, levee hands in the throes of the blues, cowboys singing down their herds, barroom loafers howling for sweeter women, Irish section hands wanting to go home, hoboes making fun of Jay Gould's daughter. The characters are real as life, only more lyric than life ever quite gets to be.[86]

Sandburg accompanied himself on a guitar with no additional musicians singing or playing instruments. He strummed with two fingers and stayed basically within two keys, A and C. Even after classical guitar icon Andrés Segovia gave Sandburg a few lessons and composed a little practice piece, writing "for my dear Sandburg to teach his fingers as if they were little children,"[87] Sandburg's style remained simple but perfectly matched to his delivery. He sarcastically said of his playing, "If I'd gotten a prison sentence, I'd probably have become pretty good on the guitar."[88] Sandburg dedicated a poem to Segovia, titled "The Guitar," which Sandburg described as:

A small friend weighing less than a newborn infant, ever responsive to all sincere efforts aimed at mutual respect, depth of affection or love gone off the deep end. A device in the realm of harmonic creation whose six silent strings have the sound potential of profound contemplation or happy-go-lucky whim.[89]

Sandburg became more and more in demand on stages and in halls across America, often performing for three or

more months at a time. By the late 1920s, Sandburg esti-
mated that he had performed at about two-thirds of the
state universities in the country. In the fall of 1936, he gave
thirty platform performances in seventy days, traveling
through a dozen states and Canada.

In a letter to President Franklin D. Roosevelt in 1938,
Sandburg told the president to "expect me someday at the
White House door with guitar, for an evening of songs and
of stories from the hinterlands."[90] During the 1950s while
he was in his seventies, Sandburg continued to perform
extensively. He gave concerts to an audience of 9,000 at the
University of California and performed in front of 3,000
admirers at the Genial Federation of Women's Club in
Asheville, North Carolina. He was so much in demand that
he turned down hundreds of invitations each year, holding
sacrosanct time for his poetry, biography, journalism, and
other pursuits, regardless of monetary considerations. Sandburg's reach was extended further by the release of twelve
records of his singing folk songs.

The American Songbag

Sandburg was nearly fifty years old when he published
The American Songbag in 1927. He considered this to be
the most difficult book he had ever undertaken. The effort
kept him tied down long past his expectations, and it wore
him out—physically, mentally, and emotionally. The book
quickly became a standard in households across America, and it remained in print continuously for more than
seventy years.

The book contained lyrics, piano accompaniment, and historic commentary for 280 folk songs—100 of which had never been published before. Sandburg sorted songs into chapters by subject matter, which illustrate the wide range of the work (e.g., "Minstrel Songs," "Prison and Jail Songs," and "Darn Fool Ditties"; geographical spreads, including "Great Lakes and Erie Canal," "Mexican Border Songs," and "Southern Mountains"; and historical timeframes, including "The Ould Sod," "Revolutionary Antiques," and "Pioneer Memories.")

Sandburg dedicated the *Songbag* "To those unknown singers—who made songs out of love, fun, grief—and to those many other singers—who kept those songs as living things of the heart and mind—out of love, fun, grief."[91] He called the book "an All-American affair, marshaling the genius of thousands of original singing Americans." He understood that in the songs and saying of a people there is truth—an expression of the national character and wisdom at its most common level.[92] He combines folk song with poetry in his poem "Singing****" (note: Sandburg used the "N" word in the title and text of the poem, which was commonly accepted in early twentieth-century America).

YOUR bony head, Jazbo, O dock walloper,
Those grappling hooks, those wheelbarrow
    handlers,
The dome and the wings of you, ****,
The red roof and the door of you,
I know where your songs came from.
I know why God listens to your, "Walk All Over
    God's Heaven."

I heard you shooting craps, "My baby's going to
    have a new dress."
I heard you in the cinders, "I'm going to live
    anyhow until I die."
I saw five of you with a can of beer on a summer
    night and I listened to
      the five of you harmonizing six ways to sing,
      "Way Down Yonder
      in the Cornfield."
I went away asking where I come from.[93]

Such songs and Sandburg's poetry chronicled the cus-
toms and lives of the American melting pot. He writes in
the introduction to *The American Songbag* that:

> There is a human stir throughout the book with
> the heights and depths to be found in Shakespeare.
> A wide human procession marches through these
> pages. The rich and the poor; robbers, murders,
> hangmen; fathers and wild boys' mothers with
> soft words for their babies; workmen on railroads,
> steamboats, ships; wanderers and lovers of homes,
> tell what life has done to them.[94]

In 1950, at age seventy-two, Sandburg published a
second edition, which included many new songs and an
introduction written by Bing Crosby. He titled it the *New
American Songbag.*

The *Songbag* first published many tunes now consid-
ered folk song standards, including the "Ballad of the Boll
Weevil," "C.C. Rider," "The John B. Sails," "The Weaver,"
"Casey Jones," "Shenandoah (as the Wide Mizzoura),"

"Mister Frog Went A-courting," "The Farmer (Is the Man Who Feeds Them All)," "Hangman," "Railroad Bill," "La Cucaracha," "Hallelujah, I'm a Bum," "Midnight Special," "The House Carpenter," and "Frankie and Johnny."

These songs first inspired such legends as the Weavers, Woody Guthrie, and Burl Ives, and later on, the Kingston Trio, Pete Seeger, Leadbelly, and the New Lost City Ramblers. Later twentieth-century folk, popular music, rock, and country music artists also recorded songs from the *Songbag*. Among these were the Beach Boys, Johnny Cash, the trio of Peter, Paul, and Mary, Creedence Clearwater Revival, Dan Zanes, Joan Baez, and Bob Dylan.

The Songbag established Sandburg as a critical advocate for the preservation and collection of folk songs and as a performer who taught America its songs. In the introduction to the 1927 book, he describes how the songs resonated with all levels of society.

> This whole thing is only in its beginning, America knowing its songs . . . It's been amazing to me to see how audiences rise to 'em; how the lowbrows just naturally like Frankie an' Albert while the highbrows, with the explanation that the murder and adultery is less in percentage than in the average grand opera, and it is the equivalent for America of the famous gutter song of Paris—they get it.[95]

In the introduction to the 1990 edition of *The American Songbag*, Garrison Keillor wrote that "Sandburg was a cultural patriot who came along at a time when he was needed."[96] Bob Dylan, who visited the elderly Sandburg in 1964, acknowledged that he was following the path blazed by Sandburg so many years before. Dylan would go on to win the Nobel Prize in Literature in 2016 for having created new poetic expressions within the great American song tradition—a tradition preserved and expanded by the foundational work of Sandburg some one hundred years earlier.

Chapter Seven

A Walk in the Woods with Nature's Poet

Above all, Sandburg and family loved to walk in the woods. Fresh air and long, rugged walks provided them with freedom, inspiration, and energy all their lives. He declared that:

> [F]reedom is found, if anywhere, in the great out-door world of wild breezes and sunshine and sky. . . . To get out into the daylight and fill your lungs with pure air, to stop and watch a spear of grass swaying in the wind, to give a smile daily at the wonder and mystery of shifting light and changing shadow, is to get close to the source of power.[97]

Everywhere the Sandburgs lived, they walked: from early days in Galesburg—where a working-class youth had no choice but to walk—to rural Wisconsin, houses in the Chicago suburbs, the lakefront property in Michigan, and their North Carolina farm. During Carl and Paula's few months of courtship, biographer Penelope Niven notes:

> [Paula] liked to walk in all weather, and could be seen even on rainy days striding briskly through

the elegant prairie community apparently heedless of the splash of mud on her skirts. . . . Even in ice or snow she would walk from her boardinghouse to the refuge of the woods. . . . On sunny days, Paula often took school work to do, books to read or letters to write in the woods.[98]

In a 1908 letter to Paula, Carl casts a hike in more poetic terms:

Back from a long hike again—sand and shore, night and stars and this restless inland sea— Plunging white horses in a forever recoiling Pickett's charge at Gettysburg—On the left a ridge of jaggedly outlined pines, their zigzag jutting up into a steel-grey sky—under me and ahead a long brown swath of sand—to the right the ever-repelled but incessantly charging white horses and beyond an expanse of dark—but overall, sweeping platoons of unguessable stars! Stars everywhere! Blinking, shy-hiding gleams—blazing, refulgent beacons—an infinite, travelling caravanserie— going somewhere![99]

In a letter to Carl, Paula shares that she has "walked abroad my two hours today! Am returned to natural life— out-door—etc.—You'll see how strong I'll be when you get back."[100] In another letter, Carl noted that "he was hard as hickory from his year-around passion for long walks out-doors—sometimes twenty miles or more a day."[101]

Sandburg took city treks as well. After a busy day, Gregory d'Alessio (a New York City syndicated cartoonist, painter, and classical guitar enthusiast) hoped that Sandburg would forget for once his mania for walking, especially late at night along empty streets. A yellow checkered cab was flagged, but Sandburg waved it on, saying to d'Alessio, "I don't mind; you've had a hard night. But this fresh air will do you good!"[102]

The Sandburg family lived their last two decades at Connemara. Two lakes, two peaks (named Little Glassy and Big Glassy), and paths along the barn, house, garden, and other buildings highlight the five miles of hiking trails there. Paula noted:

> [W]e found that our land goes over the top of Little Glass Mt and up to the very top of Big Glass Mt—at least a mile of real climbing from the house. The timber seems endless—mostly oak, black gum, yellow pine, white pine, hickory— with dogwood everywhere. The hills will be white with dogwood blossoms in Spring. There are many trails and paths through the mountain— perfect for horseback riding. We walked up and down the mountain for 3 hours—a perfect day— air crisp and windy! How Dad will enjoy these walks! From the top of Big Glassy you see all over Hendersonville and the country about, Smokies and Blue Ridge. A far wider view than that from our porch. And in every direction, you are on top of the World![103]

The Sandburgs walked or rode horses over Big Glassy and Little Glassy, and as biographer Harry Golden notes, they often sang as they went "bringing back to the house stones or nuts or leaves whose shapes or colors pleased us, or pieces of wood that reminded us of some bird in flight or a creature we had once met in a dream."[104] Just down from the top of Little Glassy, youngest daughter Helga and Carl named a limb that seemed to have a great snout, an open mouth, and eye—the Dragon Limb. Granddaughter Paula remembered, "The children looked on it with some awe and trod the dragon's domain with respect."[105] More than seventy years later, the limb can still be found but now extends much farther across the trail.

Sandburg's collection of thirty or forty walking sticks—mostly gifts from his many admirers—can still be seen on display at Connemara. For his long walks along its mountain trails, however, he carried an ax and chopped away at branches and dead wood along the way. Sandburg reflects on legs and life in the poem, "The Walking Man of Rodin":

> LEGS hold a torso away from the earth.
> And a regular high poem of legs is here.
> Powers of bone and cord raise a belly and lungs
> Out of ooze and over the loam where eyes look
> and ear hear
> And arms have a chance to hammer and shoot
> and run motors.
> You make us
> Proud of our legs, old man.
> And you left off the head here,
> The skull found always crumbling neighbor of the
> ankles.[106]

Nature's Poet

Of the one thousand poems in *The Complete Poems of Carl Sandburg*, at least 10 percent refer to an aspect of nature in their titles: times of day, the seasons, weather, geographical features, plants, and animals. In "Daybreak," Sandburg explains that "Night is getting ready to go / And Day whispers, 'Soon now, soon.'"[107] In "Stars," Sandburg notes that they "are too many to count," and they "tell nothing—and everything." And that stars "are so far away they never speak when spoken to. Stars are priceless yet paid for."[108]

In "Falltime," he describes the "cold of a ripe oat straw, gold of a southeast moon, Canada thistle blue and flimmering, larkspur blue."[109] In "Autumn Movement," he "cried over beautiful things knowing no beautiful thing lasts," and explains that:

> The northwest wind comes and the yellow is
>   torn full of
> holes, new beautiful things come in the first
>   spit of
> snow on the northwest wind, and the old
>   things go,
> not one lasts.[110]

Frost, rain, wind, snow, and fog attracted Sandburg's imagination. Although he never saw himself as a member of the Imagists School (founded by Sandburg's friend and poet Ezra Pound to rail against romanticism and Victorian poetry), he was influenced by their orientation toward poetry—the elimination of unnecessary words and the use of concrete images. Professor Hazel Durnell praises the best known of these poems, "Fog," for its "airy fantasy, grace and pleasing imagery," and said that the poem gave Sandburg recognition "as a master of metaphor and figurative speech."[111]

> The fog comes
> on little cat feet.
>
> It sits looking
> over harbor and city
> on silent haunches
> and then moves on.[112]

Geographical features like the sea and river, mountain and valley, and meadow and prairie are other themes of Sandburg's nature poetry. In the "Young Sea," he says:

> Let only the young come,
>   Says the sea.
> Let them kiss my face
>   And hear me.
> I am the last word
>   And I tell
> Where storms and stars come from.[113]

In "Prairie," he declares that he "was born on the prairie and the milk of its wheat, the red of its clover, the eyes of its women, gave me a song and a slogan."[114] The prairie country is for Sandburg the symbol of the pioneering spirit that built America.

In "Bluebird," he gives a nod to his eldest daughter, Margaret, who constructed bluebird houses and hung them all about the farm. He notes that worms and bugs and corn, seed, and berries are only part answer to the question asked in "Bluebird": What do you feed on?[115]

Wherever the family lived, they grew flowers, and flowers were a common subject of Sandburg's poetry: lilies, foxgloves, morning glories, hydrangea, and others. In "Hydrangeas," he describes the fading flowers in the fall:

> DRAGOONS, I tell you the white hydrangeas
> turn rust and go soon.
> Already mid September a line of brown runs
> over them.
> One sunset after another tracks the faces, the
> petals.
> Waiting, they look over the fence for what
> way they go.[116]

Sandburg understood that communing with nature was essential for his creativity and renewal. He suggests that:

> A man must find time for himself. Time is what we spend our lives with. . . . If we are not careful, we find others spending it for us. . . . It is necessary now and then for a man to go away by himself and experience loneliness, to sit on a rock in the forest and ask of himself, "Who am I, and where have I been, and where am I going?". . . If one is not careful, one allows diversions to take up one's time—the stuff of life.[117]

Chapter Eight

War and Peace in Poetry and Prose

After hearing tales of Civil War battles from Uncle Joe, a veteran who rented a room in the Sandburg home, a young Carl Sandburg told his family that "war is a wonder and soldiers are a wonder. . . . I wish we had a war now and I could be a soldier."[118] Sandburg lived through three wars and fought in the Spanish-American War where he saw no direct action but suffered in the heat, wearing woolen uniforms recycled from the Civil War; he fought off malaria-carrying mosquitoes, and ate beef and beans from tin cans. He said, "It was a dirty and lousy affair while it lasted."[119]

In his poetry and prose, Sandburg explores how war affects the common soldier. He writes that "war has a thousand faces . . . and a fantastic variety of means of testing a boy's brain, for stretching his nerves, for exposing his heart or burying his heart."[120] And that "War happens inside a man. It happens to him alone. It can never be communicated. That is the tragedy—and perhaps the blessing."[121]

In the first four centuries, most followers of Christianity refused to fight in war. This pacifist tradition continued at various points in the history of religion, notably in the Reformation peace churches, such as the Quakers, and the nonviolent movements of Mahatma Gandhi and the Rev. Martin Luther King Jr., which were influential during Sandburg's life. Sandburg focused on three pacifist-linked themes: the disparity of wealth and power along socioeconomic and political lines; the horror and futility of war, especially in the modern era; and the universal humanity shared by both sides of an armed conflict.

In the lead up to America's entry into World War I, Sandburg opposed war in solidarity with the working-class movement's opposition to pro-war capitalists and ruling dynasties, not from a religious perceptive. He disparaged the German kaiser as the head of a repressive state, which deserved to be wiped off the face of the earth. In *The Other Carl Sandburg*, Philip R. Yannella writes:

> The Kaiser, always presented as part crackpot, part bloodthirsty madman, was depicted by Sandburg as "the one-armed mastoid Kaiser," the "half-cracked one-armed child of the German kings," "the child born with his head wrong-shaped," "the blood of rotted kings in his veins," "the last of quivering Hohenzollerns," and "a piece of trash."[122]

In "A Million Young Workmen, 1915," Sandburg describes the decadence of pro-war rulers:

> The kings are grinning, the kaiser and the czar— they are alive riding in leather-seated motor cars, and they have their women and roses for ease, and they eat fresh poached eggs for breakfast, new butter on toast, sitting in tall water-tight houses reading the news of war.[123]

In "And They Obey," he echoes the futility of war's cycle: commands to soldiers to "SMASH down the cities. / Knock the walls to pieces," and then to workmen and citizens all, to "Build up the cities. / Set up the walls again."[124]

Sandburg paints the desolation of war on the battlefield and on the home front, sometimes in brutal, graphic language. In "Smoke":

> Millions of men go to war, acres of them are
>   buried, guns and ships broken, cities burned,
>   villages sent up in smoke, and children where
> Cows are killed off amid hoarse barbecues vanish
>   like finger-rings of
> Smoke in a north wind.[125]

In "Killers," 16 million soldiers sleep along the picket lines:

> Some of them long sleepers for always,
> Some of them tumbling to sleep tomorrow
>   for always
> Fixed in the drag of the world's heartbreak,
> Eating and drinking, toiling . . . on a long job
>   of killing.[126]

In "Iron," the shovel and the gun are shown to be brothers.[127] And in "Grass," he laments the agonies of war too soon forgotten. The grass covers the soldiers buried in the battlefields, and in two years and again in ten years, people ask, "What place is this? Where are we now?"[128]

Sandburg believed soldiers kept "alive the names of those who left red prints of bleeding feet at Valley Forge in Christmas snow."[129] He depicted allied soldiers as clean-scrubbed, clear-eyed patriots—ready to do their duty but not eager for battle nor interested in the spoils of war. In his most famous poem from World War I, "The Four Brothers," he declares that the brother-soldiers of France, Russia, Britain, and America were common folk ready to defend their respective nations: "Cowpunchers, cornhuskers, shopmen, ready in khaki; Ballplayers, lumberjacks, ironworkers, ready in khaki."[130] The poem was read at Liberty Bond rallies across the country.

In the lead-up to America's formal entry into World War II, Sandburg opposed isolationism and supported efforts like the lend-lease program to bolster Britain's stand against Nazi Germany. He asks, if Britain falls, would that be the end of the war or just an interlude, a short breathing spell? In his article "A Long War or Short," he explains:

> For a long time now, a long time as struggle, bitter misunderstandings, suffering are measured, we shall know fog and smoke. By wish or will or national policy, can we keep out of the present war? If so, what of the one to come just after, the war to dispute would-be world conquerors who want to take us in their stride?[131]

In "Is There Any Easy Road to Freedom," Sandburg says that "in order to keep our freedoms we must never take them for granted; we must always keep threats to freedom in check."

> There are freedom shouters.
> There are freedom whisperers.

Both may serve.
Have I, have you, been too silent?
Is there an easy crime of silence?
Is there any easy road to freedom?[132]

Sandburg covered World War II in a weekly column, and he gave public speeches at rallies and on radio broadcasts. These were compiled into the 1940 book The *Home Front Memo*. It included "Wings Over Norway," describing the crown princess's support for the Royal Norwegian Air Force, which was featured in the 2021 PBS series *Atlantic Crossing*.[133] The book also includes "The Man with Broken Fingers," which is about torture at the hands of the Gestapo. Sandburg asks:

Did he think about violins or accordions he
    would never touch again?
Did he think of baby or woman hair he would
    never again play with?
Or of hammers or pencils no good to him
    anymore?
Or of gloves and mittens that would always be
    misfits?[134]

The poem reached many millions of listeners and readers. It was read during the *Treasury Hour Program* on the radio in the United States, broadcast over shortwave radio to various parts of Europe, and published in Swedish, Danish, Norwegian, and Russian.

In other writings, Sandburg describes the use of slave labor, the pull of the Hitler Youth movement, and the tragedy of book burnings. He tells how in Nazified Europe the same revered books supporting democracy that are shelved in the U.S. Library of Congress "have been put to death. With grimaces, jeers, maledictions, these books have been burned, banned, published as dead, cremated, and the epitaphs well chosen."[135]

At a national unity rally at the Chicago Stadium in 1941, 24,000 people came to hear Judy Garland sing "God Bless America" and listen to the words of Carl Sandburg. He recalled widespread boos when the song was sung at an America First rally a couple of weeks earlier. Firsters couldn't stomach an anthem written by Irving Berlin, a Jew. Sandburg warns:

> When the long arm of Nazi propaganda reaches from Berlin to Chicago and Philadelphia telling us what songs we can or can't sing, we are merely getting a little preview and foretaste of what that propaganda will hand us when its prestige and power have been fortified and buttressed to the extent we will surely see if and when the British Isles become a Nazi outpost, we will surely, regret the lack of what we might have determined to send.[136]

Other *Home Front* articles trace battlefield campaigns, review war production and new weapons, and warn of the dangers of propaganda and spies. He implores readers to be mindful of "the factor of fate, the unforeseen event which makes any fixed date for the end of the war just a guess, a blind estimate, picking the winner of a county-fair horse race in heavy mud."[137]

Sandburg emphasized the importance of pulling together as a nation:

> We have seen conscription, taxes, rationing, wherein we didn't volunteer but the government told us how and when. In the main, considering what a big country we are and how many scattered millions have been told how to regulate their lives, the war measures have worked out fairly well. In the main, we have "volunteered" to go along, "free and willing."[138]

To describe the aftermath of war, Sandburg uses the image of a vast caldron:

> When after a time the heat is gone and the fire cooled and living men take a look at the then quiet caldron, they may say it was material resources that decided what came—or they may say the controlling element was the invisible motives in the hearts of men.
>
> And after the high boiling point, the deciding crisis in the caldron, there may be a long cooling-off, as hard to look at as the time of the fiercest heat.[139]

And as more deadly weapons continued to be developed during the Cold War that followed World War II, he defined the greatest threat to humanity as "The Unknown War":

> The bombs of the next war, if they control, hold the Unknown blasts—the bacterial spreads of the next war, if they control, reek with the Unknown—the

round-the-curve-of-the-earth guided missiles of the next war, should they control, will have the slide and hiss of the Unknown—the cosmic rays or light beams carrying a moonshine kiss of death, if and when they control, will have the mercy of the sudden Unknown.[140]

Sandburg provides an existential answer to war in "Sometimes they'll give a war and nobody will come."

> The little girl saw her first troop parade and asked,
>   "What are those?"
> "Soldiers."
> "What are soldiers?"
> "They are for war. They fight and each tries to kill
>   As many of the other side as he can."
> The girl held still and studied.
> "Do you know . . . I know something?"
> "Yes, what is it you know?"
> "Sometimes they'll give a war and nobody will
>   come."[141]

Chapter Nine

Child-Heart: Poetry and Prose for Children

Sandburg wrote poetry and prose for young people and grown-ups who are young at heart. His interest in writing for children began with the births of his own children—Margaret in 1911, Janet in 1916, and Helga in 1918. He penned poems about and for them. "In your blue eyes, O reckless child," he wrote in the poem "Margaret, "I saw today many little wild wishes, / Eager as the great morning."[142] And in "Child Moon," he captures Margaret's fascination with the moon, a "far silent yellow thing / Shining through the branches / Filtering on the leaves a golden sand, / Crying with her little tongue / 'See the moon!'"[143] In "Baby Toes" and "Helga," Sandburg writes about the choices his other daughters, Janet and Helga, will make and of the futures they may realize.

Baby Toes

There is a blue star, Janet,
Fifteen years' ride from us,
If we ride a hundred miles an hour.

There is a white star, Janet,
Forty years' ride from us,
If we ride a hundred miles an hour.

Shall we ride
To the blue star
Or the white star?[144]

Helga

The wishes on this child's mouth
Came like snow on marsh cranberries;
The tamarack kept something for her;
The wind is ready to help her shoes.
The north has loved her; she will be
A grandmother feeding geese on frosty
Mornings; she will understand
Early snow on the cranberries
Better and better then.[145]

And, for his granddaughter in "Second Sonata for Karlen Paula," the poet suggests that she "Try standing in the sun telling your shadow, / 'I like you much—you never fail me.'"[146]

When Sandburg first began to create prose stories for children, his family consisted of two young daughters and one baby girl. He tested stories by asking the girls to choose the ones they wanted to hear again. He called his daughters the "Homeyglomeys" and gave each a nickname—"Spink" for Margaret, "Skabootch" for Janet, and "Swipes" for Helga. It must have tickled the girls when they saw their nicknames being used in the stories he would later publish. Sandburg wrote that his kids were "a loan, only a loan, out of nowhere, back to nowhere, babbling, wild-flying—they die every day like flowers shedding petals—and come on again."[147]

Rootabaga Stories

After the existential horror and futility of World War I, Sandburg turned his writings to topics that offered him more hope and creative possibilities than that offered by his work as an overseas war correspondent or his labor and crime beat with the *Chicago Daily News*. He chose to write prose literature for children, which he dedicated to "the eternal child, who, when he or she hears language spoken, hears rhythm, not sense."[148] The tales provided the respite he sought from the intense years "of too much propaganda and not enough fun."[149] He called them his "refuge from the imbecility of a frightened world."[150] Sandburg found liberating truth in these landscapes of fantasy; although, between the lines are glimpses of the struggles of life as old agrarian values fade with no clear substitutes for an emerging urban way of life.

Sandburg published several books of interrelated short stories, beginning with *Rootabaga Stories* in 1922, followed by a sequel, *Rootabaga Pigeons* in 1923, and a lesser-known volume, *Potato Face* in 1930. And twenty-five years after Sandburg's death, a collection of previously unpublished stories was published as *More Rootabagas* in 1993. Sandburg's playful title, "Rootabaga(s)," was taken from the rutabaga—a big, lumpy yellow turnip. As a boy in Galesburg, Sandburg ate rutabagas, and each fall at the county fair, he looked on with admiration as the blue ribbon was being awarded to the best one.

By February 1927, *Rootabaga Stories* and *Rootabaga Pigeons* had sold 20,000 copies. The volumes would continue to sell steadily long after Sandburg's lifetime, and they are still in print one hundred years later in 2022. Sandburg understood that to get the full measure of his stories, they must be heard as well as read. He released records in 1953, 1958, and 1961, which encompassed nearly everything in his Rootabaga publications. Additionally, excerpts from his other writings for children were compiled into three record albums after his death. Also, Rootabaga tales were dramatized in countless sketches, including those currently performed by the Vagabond Players of the Flat Rock Playhouse in North Carolina.

Sandburg's Rootabaga tales were different from the fairy tales of the Grimm Brothers or Hans Christian Andersen—typical of what was available in 1920s America. Those tales were based on the older stories from Europe: royal princes and princesses who lived in castles and danced at balls, witches and trolls who cast spells and demanded tribute from travelers, dreadful ordeals of orphans and stepchildren who triumphed against all odds, and scenes of gruesome violence that represented the world as pure good or pure evil with little space in between. Sandburg believed that American children should have stories that were suited to American ideals, people, and landscapes. He called them "nonsense stories with a lot of American fooling in them."[151]

Rootabaga Country depicted simple, working-class American characters like Jason Squiff, who wears popcorn mittens and popcorn shoes, and Blixie Bimber, a sixteen-year-old girl "with skirts down to her shoe tops."[152] Some in Rootabaga Country, like Please Gimme, even named themselves with "the first words they speak as soon as they learn to make words."[153]

The stories focus on working-class people in the cities and farms of the American heartland. In the cities, Sandburg weaves stories about bricklayers, taxi drivers, and police. Signs at elevator stops in the new skyscrapers depict the commercial life of a city: "We Buy and Sell Anything," "Fix Anything," "The World's Finest."[154] Farmers raise crops and abundant harvests of balloons with strings for roots, picked by balloon pickers on stilts. And there are thousands of lovely corn fairies—if you know how to see and hear them— dressed in overalls while helping the corn grow:

> If it is a wild day and a hot sun is pouring down while a cool north wind blows—and this happens sometimes—then you will be sure to see thousands of corn fairies marching and countermarching in mocking grand marches over the big, long blanket of green and silver. Then too they sing, only you must listen with your littlest and newest ears if you wish to hear their singing.[155]

Animals, plants, and commonplace objects can act and speak in Rootabaga Country. The countryside is populated by foxes, horses and pigs (who wear bibs), and more exotic animals, such as the flongboo, whose yellow tail lights his way when he sneaks at night on the prairie to eat flangway-ers and hangjasts. There are elm trees and booblow trees. Chinese silver skipper buckles can sometimes be found in squashes, which can "make your luck change good to bad and bad to good."[156] And necktie poppies can be picked and attached directly to shirt collars. Jack Knife and Kindling Wood's child, Splinters, marries Hot Cookie Pan. "So, whenever you find a splinter or a sliver to a shiny little shaving of wood in a hot cookie, it is the child of the Hot Cookie Pan and the girl named Splinters."[157] And a pair of skyscrapers lean toward each other, whisper secrets, and have a child—a train named the Golden Spike Limited. The child was "free to run across the prairie, to the mountains, to the sea" on the Zigzag Railroad—made that way by an invasion of zigzagging insects called "zizzies."[158]

> Millions of zizzies came hizzing with little hizzers on their heads and under their legs. They jumped on the rails with their zigzag legs, and spit and twisted with their zigzag teeth and tongues till they twisted the whole railroad and all the rails and tracks into zigzag railroad with zigzag rails for the trains, the passenger trains and the freight trains, all to run zigzag on.[159]

Rootabaga Country includes even more unusual characters such as Any Ice Today, The Northwest Wind, The Beans Are Burning, Kiss Me, and Bozo the Button Buster Busted, who points out that "When it rains now it rains umbrellas first so everybody has an umbrella for the rain afterward."[160]

Sandburg sets his stories in both fantastical and familiar landscapes: waterways like the Shampoo River and the Big Lake of the Booming Rollers; settlements like the villages of Liver and Onions and a string of ball towns, populated by ball players with names like Home Plate, Grand Slam, and Paste It on the Nose; and the watch-manufacturing town of Elgin, Illinois, where Jonas Huckabuck is a "watchman in a watch factory watching the watches."[161]

Rootabaga Country offers gentle advice for growing up—a sort of nascent, folksy philosophy for children. Often, the advice rings true to adults as well. Here is a glimpse:

Pace of life

In the box was a pair of red slippers with a gold clock on each slipper. One of the clocks ran fast. The other clock ran slow. And he told me if I wished to be early anywhere, I should go by the clock that ran fast. And if I wished to be late anywhere, I should go by the clock that ran slow.[162]

Ambition

And a secret ambition is a little creeper that creeps and creeps in your heart night and day, singing a little song, Come and find me, come and find me.[163]

Heart or head

My head tells me to carry the clock so I can always tell if I am early or late. But my heart tells me to carry a looking glass so I can look at my face and tell if I am getting older or younger. She takes the clock because her head says so, but then changes her mind because her heart tells . . .[164]

Deeper reality

Some of the people who have eyes see nothing with their eyes. They look where they are going and they get where they wish to get, but they forget why they came and they do not know how to come away . . .[165]

Like the writers of so many children's books, Sandburg emphasizes foundational learning concepts like colors, counting, and directions. In the country of the balloon pickers:

> Hanging down from the sky strung on strings so fine the eye could not see them at first, was the balloon crop of that summer. The sky was thick with balloons. Red, blue, yellow balloons, white, purple and orange balloons—peach, watermelon and potato balloons—rye loaf and wheat loaf balloons—link sausage and pork chop balloons—they floated and filled the sky.[166]

"Whenever [the Big Buff Banty Hen] . . . goes to the front door and lays an egg in the door-bell, she rings the bell once for one egg, twice for two eggs, and a dozen rings for a dozen eggs."[167] Hatrack the Horse says that "I am going away up north and west in the Rootabaga Country to see the towns different from each other. Then I will come back east as far as I went west, and south as far as I went north, till I am back again. . . ."[168]

Often the trickster, Sandburg plays with the meanings and sounds of words. Gimme the Ax, who has one son and one daughter, reasons, "My first boy is my last and my last girl is my first." Rags Habakuk concludes that "I will be back soon if not sooner and when I come back, I will return."[169] The Gimme the Ax family "sold everything they had, pigs, pastures, pepper pickers, pitchforks" and then left to go "to Kansas, to Kokomo, to Canada, to Kankakee, to Kalamazoo, to Kamchatka, to the Chattahoochee."[170] Hot Balloons sold "slips, flips, flicks and chicks by the dozen."[171] And, "If you want to remember the names of all six of the

Sniggers children, remember that the three biggest were named Blink, Swink and Jink but the three littlest ones were Blunk, Swunk and Junk."[172]

Rootabagians live by a clear, gentle, and dignified ethical code. Social distinctions and money are absent, although Sandburg subtly brings issues of social justice into many of the stories. The lack of a social safety net is lamented in the story of Bimbo the Snip, who meets an old widow woman scrounging kindling wood because she didn't have money to buy coal after her husband had been killed in a sewer explosion. In the story, Bevo the Hike told her, "You have troubles. So have I. You are carrying a load on your back people can see. I am carrying a load and nobody sees it."[173] In "The Dollar Watch and the Five Jack Rabbits" someone is scheduled to be hanged because "he sneezed at the wrong time and he sneezed in front of the wrong persons."[174] Another story lampoons the vanity of the very rich as witnessed by the dying rich man who:

> wanted to be remembered and left in his last will and testament a command they should build a building so high it would scrape the thunder clouds and stand higher than all other skyscrapers with his name carved in stone letters on the top of it, and an electric sign at night with his name on it, and a clock on the tower with his name on it.[175]

The futility, escalation, and cost of war is explored in the story "How Two Sweetheart Dippies Heard About Sooners and Boomers." In the beginning they "Told stories, spoke jokes, made songs, with their arms on each other's shoulders" but later fought wars to decide when peach pickers must pick peaches and whether "dishwashers must keep their money in pig's ears with padlocks pinched on with pincers."[176]

More Poems for Children

By the time Sandburg published his first book of poems for children, *Early Moon*, in 1930, all but one of his children were in their teens. He published another children's poetry book, *Wind Song*, in 1960, when he was eighty-two years old. He dedicated this volume to his grandchildren, John Carl and Karlen Paula. In 1962, he released *Carl Sandburg's Poems for Children*, which included more than forty poems.

These children's poems share many of the characteristics found in the Rootabaga series, especially the playfulness with the sounds and meanings of words and gentle advice for growing up. In the preface to *Early Moon*, Sandburg answers a series of questions concerning children and poetry. He suggests that children should write poetry "whenever they feel like it, starting when they first begin to speak." He continues to say that "Poems are made of words and when a child is learning to talk, to shape words on its tongue, is a proper time for it to speak poetry—if it can."[177]

Sandburg encourages children to be open to life. In "Doors" he asks, "If a door is open and you want it open / why shut it?"[178] In "Little Girl, Be Careful What You Say," Sandburg advises children to be careful (and careless) in how they use words "for words are made of syllables / and syllables, child, are made of air— / and air is so thin—air is the breath of God—."[179] In "Primer Lesson," he warns of proud words that are not easy to call back for "They wear long boots, hard boots; they / walk off proud; they can't hear you / calling—."[180] And in "Arithmetic," the poet gives multiple definitions that bring a smile and nod of understanding from both children and adults alike:

> Arithmetic is where the answer is right and every-
> thing is nice
>   and you can look out of the window and see
>   the blue sky—or the answer is
>   wrong and you have to start all over and try
>   again and see how it
> comes out this time.[181]

In a letter to Sandburg, pioneering architect Frank Lloyd Wright wrote, "All the children that will be born in the Middle West during the next hundred years are peeping at you now, Carl—between little pink fingers, smiling, knowing that in this Beauty, they have found a friend."[182] World-renowned photographer Alfred Stieglitz and his equally famous wife, the painter Georgia O'Keeffe, predicted that the Rootabaga books would find their way "into every home eventually—because of the sheer delight—the true poetry of life—the music in the modest volume."[183]

Sandburg biographer Penelope Niven writes that Sandburg came to understand that:

> [Y]oung people are young no matter how many
> years they live; that there are children born old and
> brought up to be full of fear; that a young heart
> keeps young by a certain measure of fooling as
> the years go by; that men and women old in years

sometimes keep a fresh child heart and, to the last, salute the dawn and the morning with a mixture of reverence and laughter.[184]

Sandburg loved his time with children. In "People with Proud Chins," he says:

I TELL them where the wind comes from,
Where the music goes when the fiddle is in the
    box.
Kids—I saw one with a proud chin, a sleepyhead,
    And the moonline creeping white on her pillow.
    I have seen their heads in the starlight
    And their proud chins marching in a mist of
    stars.
They are the only people I never lie to.
    I give them honest answers,
Answers shrewd as the circles of white on brown
    chestnuts.[185]

Chapter Ten

Lincoln Biographer and Historian

Best known for his monumental Lincoln biographies: *Abraham Lincoln: The Prairie Years* and *Abraham Lincoln: The War Years*, Sandburg wrote and spoke about America's Civil War president for forty years.

Sandburg and Lincoln had much in common. The lives of both were shaped by the prairies and common people of the American heartland. In *Always the Young Strangers*, Sandburg recalls hearing "the talk of men and women who had eaten with Lincoln, gave him a bed overnight, heard his jokes and lingo, remembered his silences and his mobile face."[186] Some of the oldest citizens in Galesburg were among the Lincoln generation of rugged pioneers in what was then the western frontier. These "men of failing sight and hearing . . . told of seeing virgin prairie grass that rose standing six feet high, which had roots so tough and tangles so deep they often broke the wooden plowshare that tried to break them."[187] In "Good Morning America," Sandburg pays tribute to their stoutheartedness. Pioneers who were "lean, hungry, fierce, dirty" and broke "sod for unnumbered millions to come."[188]

Sandburg and Lincoln loved to ponder the meaning of words and listen to the sounds of language. In *Abe Lincoln*

Grows Up, Sandburg wrote that the young Lincoln "was hungry to understand the meaning of words and would lay awake hours at night thinking about the meaning of language."[189] In the foreword to Sandburg's *Abraham Lincoln: The Prairie Years and the War Years*, Alan Axelrod wrote that Lincoln "enjoyed puns and folk sayings," relished "the plain homespun language of a man of the people," and enjoyed reading out loud.[190] Biographer Penelope Niven adds that Lincoln "invented words for his own use, admired brevity and economy of speech, and held in enduring affection and respect the working people from which he came."[191]

American journalist Max Lerner observed that "here was the writing of a democrat, a poet and storyteller, and earthy Midwesterner and singer of the people, who has written about another democrat who was also something of a poet in his way, a storyteller and an earthy Midwesterner and a product of the popular masses."[192] Like Lincoln, "Sandburg was a common man with an uncommon mind. He has the same ideas about America that Lincoln had,"[193] writes Hazel Durnell in *The America of Carl Sandburg*.

Lincoln barely won the popular vote in his second election, and up until the time of his death, he was denounced by nearly everyone in Washington. According to Greg Loren Durand, author of *America's Caesar: The Decline and Fall of Republican Government in the United States of America*, "These denunciations ceased with Lincoln's last breath, when the real Lincoln suddenly vanished from public record to be replaced by a figure resembling the mythical gods of Pagan Rome, more than a man."[194]

The new scholarship about Lincoln being taught when Sandburg attended Lombard College saw Lincoln as a great and valiant personality, not as a demi-god whose political tactics and vision were unerring. Lincoln was also perceived as a champion of the working class whose administration promoted such policies as the Homestead Act, Land Grant Colleges, and a graduated income tax.

In 1901, the U.S. Treasury introduced a new copper penny with Lincoln's face on the coin to honor his one hundredth birthday. In a column for the *Milwaukee Daily News*, Sandburg focused on the president's working-class roots to explain why he thought this was a good idea:

> The face of Abraham Lincoln on the copper cent seems well and proper. If it were possible to talk with that great good man, he would probably say that he is perfectly willing that his face to be placed on the cheapest and most common coin in the country. . . .
>
> Only the common people walk out of their way to get something for 9 cents reduced from 10 cents. The penny is the coin used by those who are not sure of tomorrow, those who know that if they are going to have a dollar next week, they must watch the pennies this week. . . .
>
> The common, homely fact of "Honest Abe" will look good on the penny, the coin of the common folk from whom he came and to whom he belongs.[195]

Sandburg began his Lincoln research in the 1920s and continued into the 1950s. When he started, there were only a few comprehensive collections of Lincoln materials. He searched in more than a hundred libraries and out-of-the-way bookstores and purchased thousands of books and periodicals. He examined "mountains of newspapers, letters, diaries, pamphlets, stray papers, documents, records, Congressional debates, posters, proclamations, handbills, clippings, pictures, cartoons, and memorabilia, great and small."[196] He corresponded with historians, collectors, and librarians, and interviewed the sons and daughters of Civil War political and military leaders. When he could afford clerical help, he paid a typist to copy letters and other materials, but often he did the work himself, including the sorting and resorting of tens of thousands of documents.

Books on Lincoln

Sandburg's wide-ranging research led to eight books written over thirty years: a book for children about Lincoln as a youth; a two-volume and a four-volume set that spans Lincoln's early life to his assassination; a book of selected chapters from the six volumes; and a book about Lincoln's wife, Mary. He also wrote a book about a collection of Lincoln photographs and another about a leading collector of Lincoln material. Sandburg's final book was a synthesis of his original six-volume set, augmented by new material and research.

1926   *Abraham Lincoln: The Prairie Years*

1928   *Abe Lincoln Grows Up*

1932   *Mary Lincoln: Wife and Widow*

1939   *Abraham Lincoln: The War Years*

1942   *Storm over the Land*

1944   *The Photographs of Abraham Lincoln*
        (with Frederick Hill Meserve)

1949   *Lincoln Collector: The Story of the Oliver
        R. Barrett Lincoln Collection*

1954   *Abraham Lincoln: The Prairie Years and
        the War Years*

The first book, *Abraham Lincoln: The Prairie Years*, traces Lincoln's early life up to his journey from Springfield, Illinois, to Washington to become president. The second book*, Abe Lincoln Grows Up*, chronicles Lincoln's childhood in Kentucky until his leaving home in Illinois as a young man. Sandburg initially wrote for a young audience, but his efforts soon morphed into something much more extensive and suited for an adult readership. *Abraham Lincoln: The Prairie Years* grew into a two-volume book of nearly one thousand pages. It was an immediate best seller and was serialized in the *Pictorial Review* magazine. When asked to comment on the book, Sandburg said, "There's one thing we can say for it: it is probably the only book ever written by a man whose father couldn't write his name, about a man whose mother couldn't write hers."[197]

Sandburg's first Lincoln books are more poetic and impressionist than his later works. Hazel Durnell writes that:

Sandburg's methods are those of an impressionist—vast accretions of facts, speeches, stories, individual accounts and actually recorded incidents which gradually build up the picture until it becomes the most intimately revealing interpretation of Lincoln yet produced. . . . In many places the prose of *The Prairie Years* is almost poetry.[198]

Sandburg summarized Lincoln's war years in a preface to *The Prairie Years*, but he was so caught up in the wartime stories of Lincoln that he found it difficult to stop. He labored on his next book, *Abraham Lincoln: The War Years*, for thirteen years. It was published as a four-volume set of 2,400 pages—longer than the writings of William Shakespeare and all the books of the Bible combined. When asked about his persistence, Sandburg said, "That son-of-a-gun Lincoln grows on you."[199]

It was Sandburg the seasoned journalist and historian who shaped *The War Years*. He checked all the angles of a story with multiple sources—similar to his work as an investigative news reporter. In *Carl Sandburg: A Study in Personality and Background*, Karl Detzer writes:

[Sandburg] has the reporter's knack of spotting a good story when he sees it, of knowing how to tell it in plain words, how to arrange his material to get the most dramatic value out of it, and he never bores his reader with academic stodginess. Nor is he ever guilty of carelessness with facts. Like any other good reporter, he checks and double-checks, hopes to make sure each detail is correct, each name spelled accurately.[200]

Yet, Sandburg the poet still comes through, as in passages such as this in *The War Years*:

> Yet there were moments when the processes of men seemed to be only an evil dream and justice lay in deeper transitions than those wrought by men dedicated to kill or be killed . . . Beyond the black smoke lay what salvations and jubilees? Death was in the air. So was birth. What was dying no man was knowing. What was being born no man could say.[201]

Unlike previously published biographies of Lincoln—primarily aimed at academicians and historians—Sandburg thought it more appropriate to write for a general readership, the common people. He portrays Lincoln as a leader, believing in the wisdom of the people, "let the people work through him as their organ and an instrument."[202]

Earlier biographies concentrated on Lincoln's public life, but Sandburg also probed the inner private man. Detzer wrote that Sandburg "was inside Lincoln looking out through Lincoln's eyes, seeing the world as Lincoln saw it, saying the things he would have said."[203]

American historian Charles A. Beard wrote that Sandburg also showed that Lincoln was:

> a poor limited mortal, of many moods, tempers, and distempers, stumbling blundering along, trying this and trying that, telling jokes, bewildered, disappointed, grieved by his fractious wife, weeping now, laughing then, ordering this, cancelling that, trying to smooth ruffled personalities,

looking upon mankind . . . as composed of little creatures playing and loving, quarrelling and fighting and making up again, all without much rhyme or reason.[204]

Biographer Harry Golden points out that Sandburg portrayed Lincoln as a moral force for a divided America, showing the nation what America could and morally ought to be. "It was against this background of political, economic, social, and personal forces that Lincoln kept making decisions to preserve his foremost goal—the Union—which, in its way, is the age-old goal of brotherhood."[205]

Critical reaction to Sandburg's Lincoln books was swift and divergent. Some complained that Sandburg did not adhere to formal precedent about how history should be written—especially egregious was the lack of footnotes. One reviewer said:

They are full of immensely interesting stuff but it seems to me that Sandburg has made a mess of the writing—indeed, there are plenty of places in which it must strike any reader that he is puzzled by his own material and can't figure out its significance.[206]

Others protested that Sandburg put words into Lincoln's mouth, thoughts into his head. Perhaps the most cutting comment came from famed literary critic Edmund Wilson Jr.: "There are moments when one is tempted to feel that the cruelest thing that has happened to Lincoln since he was shot by Booth has been to fall into the hands of Carl Sandburg."[207]

Supporters declared that the work was the most beautiful of all the biographies of American literature and the greatest book produced thus far along in the twentieth century. James G. Randall, a respected authority on Lincoln biographers, said that Sandburg's made all other Lincoln books "dull or stupid by comparison."[208] The American historian Charles A. Beard called the finished product "a noble monument of American literature," written with "indefatigable thoroughness."[209] Allan Nevins, known for his extensive work on the history of the Civil War, saw it as "homely but beautiful, learned but simple, exhaustively detailed but panoramic . . . [occupying] a niche all its own, unlike any other biography or history in the language."[210]

The Pulitzer Prize Board concurred with the supporters of Sandburg, awarding him the prize for history for *The War Years*. Biographer Penelope Niven said that Sandburg became Lincoln's "most visible ambassador in the twentieth century, and America knew that his name was deeply entwined with Lincoln's."[211] Sandburg augmented his Lincoln fame from his books by delivering numerous lectures in colleges and universities, making frequent television and radio performances, and writing columns, including "What Would Lincoln Do Now?" published in the *Home Front Memo*. With a nod to the conflicting issues facing President Franklin D. Roosevelt in the lead-up to World War II, Sandburg writes, "Lincoln now, if alive and effective, would often be doing the expedient thing rather than the right thing. Otherwise, he would go down politically and be swept out of use. . . ."[212]

In 1959, at the 150-year anniversary of Lincoln's birth, Sandburg became the first private citizen to address

Congress since the historian George Bancroft was invited to pay tribute to Lincoln after his assassination. Sandburg's address brought tears to many. He said, "Not often in the story of mankind does a man arrive on earth who is both steel and velvet, who is as hard as rock and soft as drifting fog, who holds in his heart and mind the paradox of terrible storm and peace unspeakable and perfect."[213]

Sandburg speaking from the rostrum of the House Chamber in 1959 with Richard Nixon and Sam Rayburn in the background.

Radio and television networks broadcasted all or part of Sandburg's address, which reached 60 million Americans. House Speaker Sam Rayburn introduced Sandburg as "the man who in all probability knows more about the life, the times, the hopes and the aspirations of Abraham Lincoln than any other human being."[214] Hazel Durnell maintained it was inevitable that Sandburg would become the literary embodiment of the Lincoln tradition. She writes:

> There occasionally arises among us one who embodies the fulfilment of American democracy, while at the same time he is the spokesman of democracy. . . . Such a man was Lincoln, and such a man is Sandburg. In his life and achievement, he stands as the proof, the very certificate, of democracy.[215]

Chapter Eleven

Affair with the Film Industry

Despite an age gap of nearly five decades, Marilyn Monroe and Carl Sandburg were good friends. He was impressed with the actress's down-to-earth personality and appreciated that Monroe, like himself, had come up the hard way. They first met either in 1958 during the filming of *Some Like It Hot* or two years later, when Sandburg was temporarily given Monroe's dressing room as his office—he called it the un-dressing room.

The two met again in 1961 at a New York apartment. When Monroe arrived late, she told Sandburg that it took longer than expected to dye her hair to look just like his. After Monroe committed suicide less than a year later, her ex-husband, Joe DiMaggio, asked Sandburg to deliver the eulogy. Ill health prevented him from doing so, but he did write a tribute for *Look* magazine, lamenting, "I wish I could have been with her that day. I believe I could have persuaded her not to take her life."216

Sandburg never earned acting credits in films or on television although his platform performances—giving lectures, reciting poetry, singing folks songs, and ad-libbing with audiences—required a carefully crafted stage persona. He was, however, a reviewer of silent films, a writer and advisor for the movies, and a celebrity on television.

At first, silent films were not considered legitimate theater by the tradition-bound students of the professional stage. Many of the early films focused on issues important to immigrant audiences who attended inexpensive nickelodeon theaters to improve their English skills and better understand American culture. Before Hollywood, Chicago was a major center for the movies: 20 percent of the world's films were made there, and the city had more theaters per capita than any other American city. The linkage of early motion pictures with immigrants and the role of silent film in Sandburg's adopted city of Chicago made the transition into films a natural step for him.

A pivotal new direction for Sandburg began in 1920 when he accepted an offer from the *Chicago Daily News* to switch from his beat as an investigative reporter to the position of staff film critic. He was already seeking something with more life and hope after the dark days of World War I, and this new venture hit the mark. A turn to children's literature completed the change. Biographer Penelope Niven writes that:

> As journalist and poet Sandburg had painted his times as he saw them, for better or worse. Now he chose to move from one kind of truth to another, from the wrenching reality of "Liars" and "Hoodlums" and the Chicago Race Riots to the fictional truth of fairy tales and motion pictures. It was a sweeping change, pivotal in his career.[217]

Sandburg quickly became a passionate advocate for photoplays, as silent movies were then called. All the great silent movie stars like Charlie Chaplin, Tom Mix, Douglas

Fairbanks, Lillian Gish, Rudolph Valentino, and Clara Bow traveled to Chicago to promote their films. Sandburg interviewed them all there and made trips to Hollywood as well. He would typically watch and write reviews for six movies on a Sunday for his column the following Saturday. This routine left time for poetry, the presentation circuit, children's books, and his early Lincoln work. From 1920 to 1928, he penned more than two thousand film reviews.

Sandburg found value in all kinds of movies—from art films and psychological dramas to action-paced Westerns, zany comedies, and novelty films. His reviews were more commentary than criticism. If it was "drammer, solid melo-drammer," or if it achieved its purpose of "delivering thrills . . . good solid melodrammer thrills," he gave it a thumbs-up.[218] He was critical, however, if the screen play, cinematography, or acting was out of place. He urged moviemakers to "let the roughnecks appear with their necks rough."[219]

For Sandburg, films were meant to be enjoyed. He steered readers toward the good movies and away from what he considered the bad ones. Sometimes he surveyed audiences to get their thoughts about a film and would then include their comments in his reviews. He also found ways to comment about current affairs such as the death penalty, assimilation of immigrants into American life, equal pay regardless of race, and the availability of information about birth control.

Sandburg often plowed new ground in his film criticism. He described the expanding reach and scope of motion pictures, and their vast potential. He theorized that films required different forms of writing and directing, and he explained the evolving technical aspects of filmmaking.

He recognized the complexities of filmmaking and the challenges of gaining favor from audiences. In the review "'Story's the Thing' Says One in the Work," he observes that:

> The industry is peopled with clever talented artists, but the demands upon them are appalling. The making of a film is as arduous a task as the producing of a stage play, but if only five out of 60 stage plays are successful, the theater-going public is satisfied. In pictures, however, audiences demand a hit every week. The scenario writer is in Babe Ruth's quandary. Babe is great as long as he makes home runs.[220]

Just as Sandburg helped introduce the wonders of the world through his sales of stereoscopic disks, he envisioned that movies would deliver educational content to schools, universities, and homes. In "What the Ocean Hides," he notes that many motion picture theaters consider no week's program complete unless it includes a newsreel, a scenic short, or an educational feature. In "Ain't Nature Wonderful in New Science Films," Sandburg reviewed a documentary about raising goats, foreshadowing later events in his own family.

He wanted society to recognize the immense implications of this new media. In "The Movies Are," he writes:

> The cold, real, upstanding fact holds—the movies are. They come so close to pre-empting some functions hitherto held exclusively by the school and university systems that the philosopher of civilization who doesn't take them into consideration

with broad, sympathetic measurement is in danger of being in the place of the drum major of the band who marched up a side street while the band went straight along the main stem—without leadership.[221]

Sandburg pictured new roles in motion pictures for writers, directors, and technicians. In "Why Scenarios Go Wrong," he advises:

Don't write stories to be read. Write movie stuff. Write what the director should direct and the actors act. A movie story is not read in a book; it is seen on a screen . . . write it as action and mummery to be played and seen.[222]

He postulates that the "director is to a film what a writer is to a novel,"[223] and he challenged filmmakers to create intelligent, challenging works. He also reports on dramatic cinematic breakthroughs such as Technicolor, Phonofilm, and the Stereoscopic Vitaphone. In "Colossal Effort Devoted to Picture Production," he explains:

Producing a picture of consequence no longer means a few days' session with a camera in a shack, as in the old days of the game. Even an ordinary picture now means an indefinite preparation, an extreme range of technical accessories, an outlay comparable to an average man's life earnings, and a regiment of mechanics and actors. . . . In its own field the cinema has its Roosevelt dams, its pyramids and its Woolworth buildings.[224]

In the 1920s, film stars often portrayed a more open and loose society: Clara Bow, with her short skirts and openly seductive behavior, and Rudolph Valentino, the swashbuckling hero who left women swooning and men copying his Latin machismo hairstyle. Many in society feared that motion pictures were leading America down a depraved road of sex and sin. Censorship boards across the country prohibited films suggesting that illicit sex, crime, or gambling was attractive. Censors held that the authority of public officials, officers of the law, and religious leaders could not be questioned. In "How Censors Differ in Thought and Deed," Sandburg points out the lack of consistent standards for the various censorship boards operating across the country:

> Censors are different from each other. Censors have temperament. Censors may or may not think there are fixed, unchangeable laws, gauges and standards by which products of the human are to be interpreted and stamped "good," "bad."[225]

Some early films did, however, reinforce racial stereotypes with impunity. In his review on D. W. Griffith's *The Birth of a Nation*, Sandburg writes that the film "has a peculiar standing among motion picture plays. There is probably no other photoplay that rates so high as an artistic production which at the same time has so low a rating as history."[226] The film was based on the novel *The Clansman*, which portrayed the Clan as heroic and newly freed slaves as servile or dangerous.

William S. Hart, Tom Mix, and Rin-Tin-Tin were among Sandburg's favorite stars, and he was a champion of

D. W. Griffith's directing abilities. But above all, Sandburg found Charlie Chaplin's art highly original and entertaining, and he judged Chaplin's *The Kid* a masterpiece. "As an artist he is more consequential in extent of audience than any speaking, singing, writing or painting artist today,"[227] wrote Sandburg. Chaplin and Sandburg were personal friends, sometimes watching movies together and staying at each other's homes. Sandburg gave Chaplin first editions of his books, and Chaplin gave Sandburg an autograph, which he had written on a drawing of a caricature of himself with hat, shoes, cane, and gloves. Sandburg returned the favor with the poem, "Without the Cane and the Derby (For C. C.)," which concludes:

> The lights are snapped on. Charlie, "the
> marvelous urchin, the little
> genius of the screen " (chatter it with a
> running monkey's laughter
> cry) Charlie is laughing a laugh the whole
> world knows.
> The room is full of cream yellow lights. Charlie is
> laughing . . . louder
> . . . lower . . .
> And again the heartbeats laugh . . . the human
> heartbeats laugh. . . .[228]

Consultant and Script Writer in Hollywood

Sandburg got his first opportunity to work directly in the movie industry in 1929, two years after his *Abraham Lincoln: The Prairie Years* was published. Silent-era movie mogul D. W. Griffith wanted Sandburg to consult on his upcoming cinematic biography of Abraham Lincoln. Sandburg's salary demand of $30,000, however, was steeper than what Griffith wanted to pay, and Sandburg didn't want the distraction from his other endeavors. More than fifty years later, a film based on Sandburg's Lincoln biographies was produced in a 1976 TV miniseries titled *Lincoln*, starring Hal Holbrook.

Sandburg had two opportunities in the 1940s to work directly in filmmaking. The first was to write and narrate the war documentary *Bomber*. The second was to write an epic novel about the American spirit for Metro-Goldwyn-Mayer, which planned to turn it into a blockbuster patriotic movie. The studio wanted him to finish in nine months, but it took a full five years, and the novel, called *Remembrance Rock*, was much too long for a film adaptation.

Assisting in writing the script for *The Greatest Story Ever Told* was Sandburg's last opportunity to work directly with motion pictures. Director George Stevens offered $125,000 for six months, but Sandburg ended up spending a year and a half in Hollywood. Although his contributions to the film were negligible, he enjoyed the stay.

Celebrity on Television

Later in life, Sandburg appeared on many early television shows as a celebrity guest for hosts such as John Daly, Ed Sullivan, Howard K. Smith, Dave Garroway, Steve Allen, Milton Berle, and Gary Moore. During the same period, his image was featured on the cover of *Life*, *Time*, *Newsweek*, *Parade*, *Wisdom*, and other magazines. The renowned film star Gene Kelly danced on television to words written by

Sandburg. A one-act opera based on *The People, Yes* was broadcast over CBS radio, starring Burl Ives and Everett Sloane. The play *World of Carl Sandburg*, starring Bette Davis, played on Broadway and toured for seventeen weeks across the country.

Radio came to Connemara in 1950 when Fred W. Friendly of CBS asked Sandburg to appear on *Hear It Now*. The production crew that came to record interviews with him included Edward R. Murrow and Joseph Wershba. Wershba brought a bottle of Old Forester bourbon with him in hopes of avoiding goat's milk, but when he tried the milk, he liked it. Friendly and Murrow returned to Connemara in 1954 to film for television an episode of their news magazine show *See It Now*. Sandburg admired Murrow's exposé of Senator Joseph McCarthy during an earlier broadcast, sending his stamp of approval with the message: "There's a lot wrong with America, Ed, but it ain't you."[229]

During his time at Connemara, Murrow asked Sandburg to name the worst word in the English language. Sandburg replied, "Exclusive—when you're exclusive, you shut out a more or less large range of humanity from your mind and heart—from your understanding of them."[230] Murrow also asked him whether he wanted to be known as a poet, biographer, or historian. Sandburg replied, "I'd rather be known as a man who says, 'What I need mainly is three things in life, possibly four: To be out of jail, to eat regular, to get what I write printed, and then a little love at home and a little outside.'"[231]

On the forty-fifth anniversary of Sandburg's death in 2012, *The Day Carl Sandburg Died* aired on the PBS American Masters series. The documentary crew returned to Connemara to examine Sandburg's life, work, and controversial legacy from a modern perspective. The film featured poetry, folk songs, and original interviews by Helga Sandburg Crile (Sandburg's youngest daughter), singer Pete Seeger, writer Studs Terkel, biographer Penelope Niven, and others.

Sandburg's groundbreaking and varied forays into the film industry extended over nearly fifty years from the 1920s to the 1960s. Whether as a movie critic, screenwriter, or celebrity guest (or as a platform artist), Sandburg, at heart, was a performer. He always played himself.

Chapter Twelve

Creating a Home Away from Home for the Eternal Hobo

A t a time when very few Americans attended college and almost none of these were women, Carl's wife, then named Lilian Steichen (later, best known as Paula Sandburg), graduated with honors from the University of Chicago. She was a strong writer and speaker and knew four languages. She had started a career in high school teaching but "as soon as she discovered his [Sandburg's] uniqueness and her great love for him, she immediately decided that she would subordinate herself to his work and needs."[232] Carl supported her choice, saying, "What the hell do I care whether you go in for literary work or not . . . I would rather be a poem like you than write poems."[233]

Paula participated in all the major decisions of Carl's career. She kept a place in their home quiet for his work; she served as a buffer, protecting Carl from the many people who vied for his attention—especially after he rose to fame. She kept the books, sometimes proofed drafts for publications, and assisted in scheduling appearances. And she kept the home place stable, raising the family during Carl's many months on the road and freeing him from many of life's mundane details.

During his extensive travels, Carl was more comfortable and productive with something close to what Paula provided back home. Many hosts provided this home away from home that he treasured. In particular, he relied on long-term hosts who sometimes shared their homes for weeks at a time, often with visits over several decades. Two of these, Lilla S. Perry and Gregory d'Alessio, wrote books about their time with Sandburg, *My Friend Carl Sandburg* and *Old Troubadour: Carl Sandburg with His Guitar Friends*, respectively.

Perry met Sandburg during an American Library Association convention where he was speaking. Perry was a member of the Friday Morning Club in Los Angeles—the second largest women's club in the country with a membership of more than three thousand. The club had already hosted Sherwood Anderson and William Butler Yeats. At Perry's encouragement, Sandburg made his debut with the club in 1920. He said, "It wouldn't seem natural to camp anywhere when I'm in Los Angeles except with the Perrys. . . . I feel at home around here. They know my ways. They let me come and go. They make no plans for me that I have to tie in with."[234]

In 1948, almost three decades after Perry met Sandburg, Gregory d'Alessio (a New York City syndicated cartoonist, painter, and classical guitar enthusiast) heard a stranger's voice on the telephone say, "I hope the guitar gang is free tonight. If so, what are the chances of getting together? This is Carl Sandburg."[235] This marked the beginning of a unique musical, literary, artistic, and social association lasting until the mid-1960s. D'Alessio describes Sandburg's first visit:

Standing there at the open door, he held in each hand a bulging shopping bag, the weight shown in the rigidity of his arms, the tautness of the bag handles, and the prominence of the veins standing out on the tops of his brown-freckled hands. The luggage contained all his needs of a longish stay: shirts (all white, but one, which was a heavy plaid), long johns, socks, hankies; and for his immediate needs, a dozen oranges, a quart of goat's milk, a fifth of Jack Daniels, and books.[236]

D'Alessio said of his hosting experience that:

Any friend of Carl Sandburg's whoever was his host knows that as a house guest, he was not a problem. You found out quickly how easy he was to feed, to entertain; you saw how well he could take care of himself, how Spartan were his needs. Then your anxiety to make good as the host of a truly great man faded away. He made you feel at home . . . when he would say to us from time to time, "You're not what's wrong with the world," we believed him.[237]

Sandburg often worked through the night until early morning when he slept for six hours or so. Perry recounts a similar pattern when Sandburg stayed with her: "He kept a newspaperman's hours, I am sure, for he never appeared for breakfast the next morning until eleven or after. At this irregular hour I got his breakfast myself, not wishing to disturb the cook's routine. These breakfasts were to me the most interesting."[238]

Sandburg liked simple accommodations and home-cooked food, and found it difficult to work in luxurious surroundings. On one occasion, he called Perry while already in Los Angeles:

> Lilla, MGM has asked me to come out here to write a novel which they want to put into a movie . . . But they've put me up here at this Casa Del Mar at the studio's expense, and I find I can't write a word. Isn't there a corner for me at your house, Lilla? I've been here three days now in all this elegance and I can't do a lick of work here. I've stared at the walls, unable to get a line on paper. I've always been able to work at your house. Can't you find a spot for me?[239]

Rather than stay at a hotel to prepare for an address at George Peabody College for Teachers in Nashville, Tennessee, Sandburg asked a graduate student, Gordon Link, "to protect me from dowager dames."[240] Link secreted Sandburg in his dormitory room for almost a full week. They stayed up far into night discussing the "New Poetry" and singing songs to the accompaniment of Sandburg's famous guitar. Link was summoned to the dean after a complaint was lodged about noise late at night. When he confessed it was Sandburg's late-night singing, the dean didn't believe him.

Both the Perry and d'Alessio families accommodated Sandburg with an upstairs room, his favorite place to write. D'Alessio expressed concern about the thirty-eight steps that the then seventy-year-old Sandburg would need to climb a few times each day. Sandburg made fun of the situation, showing d'Alessio how he could slowly navigate one step at a time; then he just scampered up. "No problem with my ticker," he said, "we got steps just like this back home in Connemara" where his study was also on the third floor.[241]

Hosts provided buffers from unwanted or unexpected guests who would demand Sandburg's time and attention. His celebrity—along with his love for home-cooked meals—was why he avoided restaurants. One evening when Perry did manage to take him to a restaurant, the waitress told Sandburg that a lady seated across the room was inquiring if he was the famous Carl Sandburg. He mischievously replied, "You can tell her that I am Robert Frost."[242] Frost was his long-time fellow poet friend who was also a senior with tousled white hair.

Hosting Sandburg often meant helping with mundane tasks, such as cashing an out-of-state check or providing a telephone in the room serving as his study. For a time, Sandburg made Donna Workman's sumptuous Chicago apartment his home base. Workman was a social activist and businesswoman who wrote a book describing what Lincoln had read during his life. Sandburg chose to stay in the smallest room for himself, which he named the Caboose. Sandburg biographer Penelope Niven describes this relationship:

> The first time he stayed there, he arrived with only a small black imitation-leather suitcase in hand and, not even a clean shirt . . . Donna and her housekeeper kept the icebox stocked with things he liked—pitchers of orange juice and tomato juice and goat's milk. All night long Donna remembered you could hear that icebox swing shut. He liked honey and coffee, pecans, and Jack Daniels.

She bought clothes for him when he needed them. Clean underwear, clean shirt . . . nice sweaters, and scarves, cashmeres. Always blues and light grays . . . Donna treated him like a baby, coddling and pampering him. She kept him supplied with vitamins, and made him get his teeth fixed by her own dentist.[243]

Occasionally, Sandburg asked his hosts to review his work and provide comment although he didn't necessarily accept friendly advice. Perry recounts the time Sandburg read an early version of a poem describing the Grand Canyon to a group of her friends:

We three listened appraisingly and critically. Then for some time we fought unavailingly to get Sandburg to remove one word we didn't like. He had used the word "spit" only one degree more or less poetic than the word expectorates, we told him. We couldn't move him. Just at that point in the verse he needed a gesture of some kind, he said, "Spit" did it.[244]

Sandburg's work sometimes required lengthy stays with or near publishers in New York, Chicago, and other cities. His publisher Alfred Harcourt invited him to stay at his new house on Long Island Sound. "There is a special place lying in a corner for you where you can comfortably have the final birth pains on the Songbag or the Lincoln or anything else that comes along and for a long time."[245] In 1939, during the editing and proofreading of the massive four volume *Abraham Lincoln: The War Years*, Sandburg lived in the Brooklyn house of Harcourt's copy editor for five months.

Sandburg Gives Back

Gregory and his wife, Terry d'Alessio (also a nationally recognized cartoonist), appreciated Sandburg's astute criticism of their work. Gregory d'Alessio writes:

> Here in our cartoon factory, he was not content to be the mere observer. He stuck his nose into my business—not as the artist, of course—but as critic, idea man, judge, editor. And he shone at it; he was canny, alert, sharp, modern, perspicacious, and best of all, jollier than my weary professional editors peering skeptically at my weekly offerings, and wantonly holding aside one out of the ten—if I was lucky—for further consideration.[246]

Sandburg sometimes invited his hosts to gala events. He escorted Lilla Perry to a special concert at the Hollywood Bowl. After the concert, Groucho Marx, Edward G. Robinson, and Kirk Douglas came by to pay their respects. On a quieter occasion, Sandburg took Perry to meet the Hollywood star Ingrid Bergman at her home for dinner. Sandburg and Bergman, both of Swedish heritage, had known each other for years and were featured in a documentary called *Swedes in America*, made in Hollywood for Sweden in 1943.

Sometimes the party came to the host's house. D'Alessio recalls, "When word got around that the poet-troubadour was to be in our midst, it was impossible to avoid a scene here like the last night of the Mardi Gras in Rio de Janeiro."[247] The parties drew a host of luminaries from publishing and the arts. Guitarists, humorists, folk singers, opera stars, and more would perform. D'Alessio shares that "Sandburg's attention toward performers at parties was not only polite and respectful, but intense with keen personal involvement. He would so enjoy a song that he would importune the singer for reprise after reprise."[248]

Sandburg's hosts soon learned that their children would be showered with his attention and affection; they became part of the extended Sandburg family. At the d'Alessios', Terry served as the den mother with Gregory as the den father. Gregory recalls that "As an added bonus to the already over-privileged little dears, they also had a den grandfather: Carl Sandburg."[249] Gregory wrote that "Kids were for him; he was for them. . . . He was kindly and entertaining, and was in turn entertained. He had lots of rewarding, grandfatherly fun with them. What a story they would tell their teachers and schoolmates the next day!"[250]

Children visiting the Flat Rock home got the Sandburg treatment as well. Long after the Sandburg grandchildren had grown up and left, Joseph Wershba (one of original producers of CBS's *60 Minutes*) and family visited the Sandburgs. Sandburg said, "The children filled, temporarily, the vast emptiness."[251] Wershba listened as his daughter and the old poet swapped nonsense words and stories. Giggling, the girls told Sandburg to "cut out that silliness." Sandburg responded pensively, "Without my silliness, I would die."[252]

Chapter Thirteen

Legacy and the Abracadabra Boys

"In number of books sold, appearances demanded, fan letters received, and honors bestowed, Sandburg was one of the most successful American poets of the century,"[253] writes biographer Penelope Niven. Between 1916 and 1967, he had at least one new book in the bookstores every two or three years. Sandburg published more than one thousand poems, penned tens of thousands of newspaper stories, and wrote more than thirty books on subjects ranging from poetry and journalism to musicology, fairy tales, biographies, and historical fiction. A complete bibliography of his works, including contributions to periodicals and anthologies, forewords, introductions, and foreign editions would number more than four hundred pages.

Sandburg received thirty-two honorary doctoral degrees. He was awarded two Pulitzer Prizes in poetry and one in history, and he was nominated for a Pulitzer in fiction. When he was nominated for a Nobel Prize in Literature in 1954, Ernest Hemingway, who won that year, said, "I would have been most happy to know that the prize had been awarded to Carl Sandburg."[254] A few years later, on his national television program, Ed Murrow asked Sandburg to comment about not winning the Nobel. Sandburg answered that he did; Hemingway had given it to him in 1954.

Portrait of Carl Sandburg on his 85th birthday.

Sandburg's honors include gold medals from the American Academy of Arts and Letters and from King Gustavus of Sweden. He was awarded a Grammy for his narration of Lincoln's letters and speeches in the composition *A Lincoln*

Portrait, won the first Albert Einstein Commemorative Award in the Humanities, and was the first white person to receive a lifetime membership from the NAACP. The states of Illinois and North Carolina declared a day in his honor, the Kennedy White House held an evening celebrating him, President Johnson awarded him the Presidential Medal of Freedom, the Postal Service issued a commemorative stamp honoring the centenary of his birth, and more than two dozen schools and colleges were named in his honor.

The twenty-first century public knows little, if anything, about the Sandburg legacy, and his accomplishments are seldom highlighted in the press or media. For example, a *Smithsonian Magazine* article about national hobo day makes no mention of Sandburg, but some of his contemporaries and colleagues are featured. A PBS documentary about Allister Cooke—a British-American writer who worked as a journalist, television personality, and radio broadcaster primarily in the United States—included a television clip of the interview he conducted during Chicago Dynamic Week with Frank Lloyd Wright and Sandburg. Even though they were sitting across from each other at a small table, Sandburg isn't mentioned or shown on the screen.

The contemporary academic assessment of Sandburg is that he is a minor figure in American literature. His poems began to slip out of high school and college anthologies in the 1950s; the last biography about Sandburg was published in 1999. From the outset of his long career, Sandburg was considered a literary outsider by the critics whom he called the Abracadabra Boys. In his poem "The Abracadabra Boys," he pokes fun at his critics and asserts that his poetry is just what he wants it to be:

Pointing at you, at us, at the rabble, they sigh and
say, these abracadabra
    boys, "They lack jargons. They fail to distin-
guish between pustules
    and pistils. They knoweth not how the kumquat
cometh."255

In the early 1900s, Sandburg's books of poetry advocated
for a struggling working class at a time when muckraking
reporters exposed the dangers of unbridled capitalism. Some
branded his poetry as propaganda. But Sandburg never shied
away from championing social justice for the working class.
Nor did he abandon free-style poetry and the use of common
speech, which he thought made his writing more accessible
to ordinary people. He didn't see this as a weakness but as an
essential part of his art and authentic to his nature.

Sandburg didn't adapt his art to the tenets of the New
Criticism that emerged in the 1920s. He didn't perceive the
formal aspects of a poem as the crucial elements that give
poetry its value, nor did he fill his poetry with obscure allu-
sions or varied levels of meaning. In a cutting review of *The
Complete Poems of Carl Sandburg*, William Carlos Williams
concludes that:

[Sandburg poetry shows] no development of the
thought, in the technical handling of the material,
in the knowledge of the forms, the art of treating
the line. The same manner of using the words, of
presenting the image is followed in the first poem
as in the last. All that can be said is that a horde
walks steadily, unhurriedly through its pages, following without affection one behind the other.256

But, of course, Sandburg's impressive array of honors proves that many scholars saw genius in his writings, and the masses who made his books best sellers were always on his side. Penelope Niven reflects on the vagaries of the critical assessment of Sandburg's works:

> Through the years, critical assessment of Sandburg the poet oscillated from praise to condemnation to, worse, dismissal and neglect. He wrote free verse when it was revolutionary, and kept at it when it went out of fashion. Eastern critics found him too provincial, Midwestern. In an age of international modernism, he was unabashedly America. In a time of nervous nationalism, he was courageous and farsighted in the outspoken global view. His passion for social justice blurred the boundary between poetry and propaganda. He wrote the "poetry of the fireside." Not the "poetry of the academy." The powerful solidarity of poets and critics in the universities diluted acceptance of the poets of "street and struggles."[257]

Niven continues to say that Sandburg set out to tell "the American nation about itself, its weakness, and strength, its past and promise. . . . Perhaps only the son of immigrants could have held so stalwartly to the national vision . . . on an epic scale, in poetry, biography and fiction."[258]

Sandburg understood these varieties of fame. He wrote:

> A man writes the best he can about what moves him deeply. Once his writing gets published as a book, he loses control over it. Time and the human

121

family do what they want to with it. It may have periods of wide reading and acclamation, other periods of condemnation, decline, neglect—then a complete fadeout—or maybe a revival. And what revives in later years is often what was neglected when new. This happens. In literature and other arts—it happens. . . .[259]

Carl Sandburg died in 1967 at age eighty-nine of natural causes. Six thousand mourners gathered at the Lincoln Memorial in Washington, D.C., to pay their respects. Ambassadors, members of Congress, Supreme Court justices, and President Lyndon B. Johnson were present. Authors Mark Van Doren and Archibald MacLeish delivered eulogies and guitarist Charlie Byrd played folksongs. The dignitaries present represented all sides of the eclectic Sandburg: social activist, political commentator and journalist; poet and philosopher; lecturer, folk singer, and musicologist; biographer and historian; children's book author; novelist; and celebrity, recording artist, and media figure.

In his eulogy, President Johnson said:

Carl Sandburg needs no epitaph. It is written for all time in the fields, the cities, the face and heart of the land he loved and the people he celebrated and inspired. With the world, we mourn his passing. It is our pride and fortune as Americans that we will always hear Carl Sandburg's voice within ourselves; for he gave us the truest and most enduring vision of our own greatness.[260]

Bibliography

Altman, Ross. "America's First Folk Singer?" *https://folkworks.org/columns/how-can-i-keep-from-talking-ross-altman/all-columns-by-ross-altman/46596-carl-sandburg-america-s-first-folk-singer*, November 15, 2018.

American Presidency Project. "President Johnson Speech at Sandburg Memorial." https://www.presidency.ucsb.edu/documents/statement-the-president-the-death-carl-sandburg.

Atlantic, The. "Those Who Make Poems," March 1942, www.theatlantic.com/magazine/archive/1942/03/those-who-make-poems/376237/, accessed May 5, 2022.

Berman, Paul, editor. *Carl Sandburg Selected Poems.* Library of America, 2006.

Bernstein, Arnie. *The Movies Are: Carl Sandburg's Film Reviews and Essays, 1920–1928.* Lake Claremont Press, 2000.

Bolin, Frances Schoonmaker, editor. *Carl Sandburg Poetry for Young People.* Sterling Children's Books, 1995.

Byrne, Kathleen. *Paula Sandburg's Chikaming Goat Herd.* Eastern National Park and Monument Association, 1993.

Callahan, North. *Carl Sandburg: Lincoln of Our Literature.* New York University Press, 1970.

Crane, St. C. Joan. *Carl Sandburg, Philip Green Wright, and the Asgard Press, 1900–1910.* University Press of Virginia, 1975.

Crowder, Richard. *Carl Sandburg*. College & University Press, 1964.

D'Alessio, Gregory. *Old Troubadour: Carl Sandburg with His Guitar Friends*. Walker and Company, 1987.

Detzer, Karl. *Carl Sandburg: A Study in Personality and Background*. Harcourt, Brace and Company, 1941.

Durnell, Hazel. *The America of Carl Sandburg*. University Press of America, 1965.

Golden, Harry. *Carl Sandburg*. The World Publishing Company, 1961.

Haas, Joseph and Lovitz, Gene. *Carl Sandburg: A Pictorial Biography*. G. P. Putnam's Sons, 1967.

Heitman, Danny. "A Workingman's Poem." *Humanities*, March/April 2013, Volume 34, Number 2 https://www.neh.gov/humanities/2013/marchapril/feature/workingmans-poet, accessed May 5, 2022.

Hendrick, George, and Henrick, Willene, editors. *Carl Sandburg Selected Poems*. A Harvest Original Harcourt, Inc., 1996.

Hendrick, George and Hendrick, Willene, editors, *Sandburg, Poems for Children: Nowhere Near Old Enough to Vote*. Alfred Borzoi Book, A. Knopf, Inc., 1999.

Hendrick, George and Hendrick, Willene, editors. *Billy Sunday and Other Poems: Unpublished, Uncollected, and Unexpurgated Works*. Harvest Original, Harcourt Brace & Company, 1993.

McCleary, Ann E. and Butler, Donna Quinn. *A History of the Carl Sandburg Home National Historic Site, 1968–2008*. National Park Service, 2016.

Meltzer, Milton. *Carl Sandburg: A Biography*. Twenty-First Century Books, 1999.

Mitgang, Herbert, editor. *The Letters of Carl Sandburg*. Harcourt Brace Jovanovich, 1968.

National Park Service. *Carl Sandburg Home: Official National Park Handbook*. Division of Publications National Park Service, 1982.

Niven, Penelope. *Carl Sandburg: Adventures of a Poet*. Harcourt, Inc., 2003.

Niven, Penelope. *Carl Sandburg: A Biography*. Charles Scribner's Sons, 1991.

Niven, Penelope. *Steichen: A Biography*. Clarkson Potter/Publishers, 1997.

Perry, Lilla S. *My Friend Carl Sandburg: The Biography of a Friendship*. Scarecrow Press, Inc., 1981.

Poetry Foundation. "Carl Sandburg." https://www.poetryfoundation.org/poets/carl-sandburg, accessed May 5, 2022.

Regan, Matthias, editor. *Carl, Sandburg: The People's Pugilists*. Charles H. Kerr, 2010.

Salwak, Dale. *Introduction to Carl Sandburg: A Reference Guide*. Self-published, 1988.

Sandburg, Carl. *Abe Lincoln Grows Up*. Harcourt Brace Jovanovich, Inc., 1928.

Sandburg, Carl. *Abraham Lincoln: The Prairie Years and the War Years*. Fall River Press, 1954.

Sandburg, Carl. *Always the Young Strangers*. Harcourt Brace Jovanovich, 1953.

Sandburg, Carl. *The American Songbag*. Harvest/HBJ Book, Harcourt Brace Jovanovich, Publishers, 1927.

Sandburg, Carl. *Breathing Tokens*. Harcourt Brace Jovanovich, 1978.

Sandburg, Carl. *Carl Sandburg's Poems for Children*. Caedmon Records-TC-1124, 1962, Vinyl.

Sandburg, Carl. *The Chicago Poems*. Dover Publications, Inc., 1916.

Sandburg, Carl. *The Chicago Race Riots*. Harcourt, Brace and Howe, Inc., 1919.

Sandburg, Carl. *The Complete Poems of Carl Sandburg Revised and Expanded Edition*. Harcourt Brace Jovanovich Publishers, 1969.

Sandburg, Carl. *Early Moon*. Harcourt, Brace and Company, 1930.

Sandburg, Carl. *Ever the Winds of Chance*. University of Illinois Press, 1983.

Sandburg, Carl. *Home Front Memo*. Harcourt, Brace and Company, 1940.

Sandburg, Carl. *Honey and Salt*. A Harvest Book Harcourt, Inc., 1963.

Sandburg, Carl. *Incidentals*. Asgard Press, 1904.

Sandburg, Carl. *Mary Lincoln: Wife and Widow.* Harcourt, Brace and Company, 1932.

Sandburg, Carl. *The People, Yes*. Harvest Book, Harcourt, Brace and Company, 1936.

Sandburg, Carl. *Potato Face*. Harcourt, Brace and Company, 1930.

Sandburg, Carl. *Rootabaga Pigeons*. Harcourt, Brace and Company, Inc., 1923.

Sandburg, Carl. *Rootabaga Stories*. Harcourt, Brace and Company, Inc., 1922.

Sandburg, Carl. *The Sandburg Range*. Harcourt, Brace and Company, 1957.

Sandburg, Carl. *Storm over the Land*. Harcourt, Brace and Company, 1942.

Sandburg, Carl. *Wind Song*. Clarion Books, 1960.

Sandburg, Helga. *A Great & Glorious Romance: The Story of Carl Sandburg and Lilian Steichen*. Harcourt Brace Jovanovich, 1978.

Sandburg, Helga. *Where Love Begins: A Portrait of Carl Sandburg and His Family as Seen Through the Eyes of His Youngest Daughter.* Donald I. Fine, Inc., 1989.

Sandburg, Margaret, editor. *Carl Sandburg Breathing Tokens: A Book of Poems.* Eastern National, 1978.

Sandburg, Margaret, editor. *The Poet and the Dream Girl: The Love Letters of Lilian Steichen and Carl Sandburg.* University of Illinois Press, 1987.

Steichen, Paula. *My Connemara: Carl Sandburg's Granddaughter Tells What It Was Like to Grow Up Close to the Land on the Famous Poet's North Carolina Mountain Farm.* Eastern National, 1969.

Stepko, Barbara. "Marilyn Monroe and Carl Sandburg—an Unlikely and Intriguing Friendship," *Vintage News,* Dec. 4, 2018. https://www.thevintagenews.com/2018/12/04/marilyn-monroe-met-carl-sandburg/, accessed May 5, 2022.

Swank, George. *Carl Sandburg: Galesburg and Beyond.* Self-published, 1983.

Villarreal, Evert. *Recovering Carl Sandburg: Politics, Prose, and Poetry After 1920.* Dissertation Submitted to the Office of Graduate Studies of Texas A&M University, August 2006. http://oaktrust.library.tamu.edu/bitstream/handle/1969.1/4167/etd-tamu-2006B-ENGL-Villarr.pdf?isAllowed=y&sequence=1, accessed May 5, 2022.

Woolley, Lisa. "Carl Sandburg and Vachel Lindsay," in *American Voices of the Chicago Renaissance.* Northern Illinois University Press, 2000.

Yannella, Phillip D. *The Other Carl Sandburg.* University Press of Mississippi, 1996.

Acknowledgments

I am indebted to Rick Rickerson, professor emeritus of language and an accomplished author, whose contributions to this book were invaluable. What started as copy edits led to a series of more substantial reviews, including the integration of content after all the chapters were complete. I greatly appreciate his personal support and sound advice about the publishing process. He helped me to become a better writer. He became a trusted friend.

I am also fortunate—especially as a first-time book author—to have found Carol and Gary Rosenberg (The Book Couple), who guided me through the final steps with competency, honesty, patience, and humor. They took the edge off what can be a daunting endeavor.

My first article about Carl Sandburg was posted on the website of the Sandburg Home National Historic Site in Flat Rock, North Carolina, with the assistance of Superintendent Polly Angelakis. Subsequent articles were published in the newsletter of the Carl Sandburg Historic Site Association in Galesburg, Illinois, by its editor, Michael Hobbs. I greatly appreciate his encouragement and his including me in conversations with the very well-informed members of the Association. Mike wrote the foreword to this book.

I also wish to express my appreciation for support from my family. My son, William Quinley, built my computer and kept it running. My son-in-law, Daniel Zimmerman, provided extensive technical support for PowerPoint presentations. My daughter, Schuyler Zimmerman, patiently listened to countless Sandburg stories and brought the grandchildren (Nate, Jack, Ben, and Allie) on multiple occasions to visit the Sandburg goats. The youngest grandson shared with a group of neighborhood kids what had become family knowledge: "If my grandpa asks you a question, the answer is always Carl Sandburg."

Endnotes

1 Niven, Penelope. *Carl Sandburg: A Biography*, 1991, p. 621.

2 Ibid., p. 621.

3 Sandburg, Carl. *Always the Young Strangers*, 1953, p. 38.

4 Crowder, Richard. *Carl Sandburg*, 1964, p. 27.

5 Sandburg, Carl. *Always the Young Strangers*, 1953, p. 230.

6 Ibid., p. 381.

7 Ibid., p. 391.

8 Ibid., p. 400.

9 Golden, Harry. *Carl Sandburg*, 1961, p. 391.

10 Sandburg, Carl. *The Complete Poems of Carl Sandburg*, 1969, p. 42.

11 Sandburg, Carl. *Ever the Winds of Chance*, 1999, p. 11.

12 Durnell, Hazel. *The America of Carl Sandburg*, 1965, p. 50.

13 Ibid., p. 49.

14 Mitgang, Herbert (ed). *The Letters of Carl Sandburg*, 1968, p. 20.

15 Sandburg, Carl. *Incidentals*, 1904, p. 26.

16 Detzer, Karl. *Carl Sandburg: A Study in Personality and Background*, 1941, p. 63.

17 Callahan, North. *Carl Sandburg: His Life and Works*, 1987, p. 45.

18 Niven, Penelope. *Carl Sandburg: A Biography*, 1991, p. 218.

19 Sandburg, Carl. *The Complete Poems of Carl Sandburg*, 1969, p. 6.

20 Sandburg, Helga. *Where Love Begins: A portrait of Carl Sandburg and his family as seen through the eyes of his youngest daughter*, 1989, p. 107.

21 Sandburg, Carl. *The Complete Poems of Carl Sandburg*, 1969, p. 3.

22 Golden, Harry. *Carl Sandburg*, 1961, p. 46.

23 Durnell, Hazel. *The America of Carl Sandburg*, 1965, p. 81.

24 Niven, Penelope. *Carl Sandburg: A Biography*, 1991, p. 55.

25 Durnell, Hazel. *The America of Carl Sandburg*, 1965, p. 72.

26 Berman, Paul (editor). *Carl Sandburg Selected Poems,* 2006, p. xxiii.

27 Poetry Foundation, "Carl Sandburg."

28 Golden, Harry. *Carl Sandburg*, 1961, p. 152.

29 Callahan, North. *Carl Sandburg Lincoln of Our Literature*, 1970, p. 49.

30 Niven, Penelope. *Carl Sandburg: A Biography*, 1991, p. 509.

31 Sandburg, Carl. *Complete Poems of Carl Sandburg*, 1969, p. 437.

32 Niven, Penelope. *Carl Sandburg: A Biography*, 1991, p. 513.

33 Ibid., p. 506.

34 Ibid., p. 506.

35 Sandburg, Carl. *The Sandburg Range*, p. 86.

36 Ibid., p. 88.

37 Niven, Penelope. *Carl Sandburg: A Biography*, 1991, p. 83.

38 Sandburg, Carl. *The Complete Poems of Carl Sandburg*, 1969, p. 258.

39 Sandburg, Helga. *A Great & Glorious Romance: The Story of Carl Sandburg and Lilian Steichen*, 1978, p. 164.

40 Ibid., p. 209.

41 Ibid., p 209.

42 Golden, Harry. *Carl Sandburg*, 1961, p. 96.

43 Sandburg, Helga. *Where Love Begins: A portrait of Carl Sandburg and his family as seen through the eyes of his youngest daughter*, 1989, p. 63.

44 Ibid., p. 63.

45 Ibid., p. 56.

46 Ibid., p. 64.

47 Niven, Penelope. *Carl Sandburg: A Biography*, 1991, p. 514.

48 Sandburg, Helga. *Where Love Begins: A portrait of Carl Sandburg and his family as seen through the eyes of his youngest daughter*, 1989, p. 65.

49 Callahan, North. *Carl Sandburg Lincoln of Our Literature*, p. 99.

50 Sandburg, Helga. *Where Love Begins: A portrait of Carl Sandburg and his family as seen through the eyes of his youngest daughter*, 1989, p. 82.

51 Steichen, Paula. *My Connemara: Carl Sandburg's granddaughter tells what it was like to grow up close to the land on the famous poet's North Carolina mountain farm*, 1969, p. 48.

52 Niven, Penelope. *Carl Sandburg: A Biography*, 1991, p. 452.

53 Callahan, North. *Carl Sandburg: Lincoln of Our Literature,* p. 49.

54 Sandburg, Carl. *The Complete Poems of Carl Sandburg*, 1969, p. 5.

55 Ibid., p. 16.

56 Ibid., p. 21.

57 Ibid. p. 12.

58 Ibid., p. 31.

59 Sandburg, Carl. *The Chicago Race Riots*, 1919, p. 56.

60 Ibid., p. xiii.

61 Golden, Harry. *Carl Sandburg*, 1961, p. 213.

62 Sandburg, Carl. *The Complete Poems of Carl Sandburg*, 1969, p. 171.

63 Sandburg, Carl. *Home Front Memo*, 1940, p. 137.

64 Ibid., p. 156.

65 Ibid., p. 157.

66 Ibid., p. 184.

67 National Park Service. *Carl Sandburg Home: Official National Park Handbook*, 1982.

68 Golden, Harry. *Carl Sandburg*, 1961, p. 30.

69 Niven, Penelope. *Carl Sandburg: A Biography*, 1991, p. 55.

70 Ibid., p. 197.

71 Ibid., p. 198.

72 Niven, Penelope. *Carl Sandburg: A Biography*, 1991, p. 186.

73 Ibid., p. 186.

74 Callahan, North. *Carl Sandburg Lincoln of Our Literature*, 1970, p. 167.

75 Niven, Penelope. *Carl Sandburg: A Biography*, 1991, p. 539.

76 Ibid., p. 539.

77 Sandburg, Carl. *Home Front Memo*, 1940, p. 38.

78 Ibid., p. 37.

79 Niven, Penelope. *Carl Sandburg: A Biography*, 1991, p. 465.

80 The American Presidency Project. "President Johnson Speech at Sandburg Memorial."

81 Niven, Penelope. *Carl Sandburg: A Biography*, 1991, p. 25.

82 Sandburg, Carl. *The Sandburg Range*, 1953, p. 125.

83 Niven, Penelope. *Carl Sandburg: A Biography*, 1991, p. 35.

84 Golden, Harry. *Carl Sandburg*, 1961, p. 79.

85 Niven, Penelope. *Carl Sandburg: A Biography*, 1991, p. 446.

86 Sandburg, Carl. *The Sandburg Range*, 1953, p. 124.

87 D'Alessio, Gregory. *Old Troubadour: Carl Sandburg with his Guitar Friends*. 1987, p. 21.

88 Ibid., p. 21.

89 Ibid., p. 26.

90 Ibid., p. 47.

91 Sandburg, Carl. *The American Songbag*, 1927, p. xii.

92 Ibid., p. xii.

93 Sandburg, Carl. *The Complete Poems of Carl Sandburg*, 1969, p. 108.

94 Sandburg, Carl. *The American Songbag*, 1927, p. xiii.

95 Ibid., p. xiii.

96 Sandburg, Carl, *The American Songbag*, 1927. p. viii.

97 Sandburg, Carl. *The Sandburg Range*, 1953, p. 120.

98 Niven, Penelope. *Carl Sandburg: A Biography*, 1991, p. 126.

99 Sandburg, Margaret, editor. *The Poet and the Dream Girl: The Love Letters of Lilian Steichen and Carl Sandburg*, 1987, p. 117.

100 Niven, Penelope. *Carl Sandburg: A Biography*, 1991, p. 189.

101 Ibid., p. 72.

102 D' Alessio, Gregory. *Old Troubadour: Carl Sandburg with his Guitar Friends,* 1987, p. 73.

103 Niven, Penelope. *Carl Sandburg: A Biography*, 1991, p. 572.

104 Golden, Harry. *Carl Sandburg*, 1961, p. 94.

105 Steichen, Paula. *My Connemara: Carl Sandburg's granddaughter tells what it was like to grow up close to the land on the famous poet's North Carolina mountain farm*, 1969, p. 117.

106 Sandburg, Carl. *The Complete Poems of Carl Sandburg*, 1969, p. 8.

107 Ibid., p. 699.

108 Ibid., p. 702.

109 Ibid., p. 88.

110 Ibid., p. 87.

111 Durnell, Hazel. *The America of Carl Sandburg*, 1965. p. 23.

112 Sandburg, Carl. *The Complete Poems of Carl Sandburg*, 1969, p. 33.

113 Ibid., p. 57.

114 Ibid., p. 79.

115 Ibid., p. 698.

116 Ibid., p. 56.

117 Niven, Penelope. *Carl Sandburg: A Biography*, 1991, p. 126.

118 Sandburg, Carl. *Always the Young Strangers*, 1953, p. 47.

119 National Park Service. *Carl Sandburg Home: Official National Park Handbook*, 1982, p. 33.

120 Durnell, Hazel. *The America of Carl Sandburg*, 1965, p. 189.

121 Ibid., p. 189.

122 Yannella, Philip. *The Other Carl Sandburg*, 1996, p. 110.

123 Sandburg, Carl. *The Complete Poems of Carl Sandburg*, 1969, p. 141.

124 Ibid., p. 40.

125 Ibid., p. 142.

126 Ibid., p. 197.

127 Ibid., p. 38.

128 Yannella, Philip. *The Other Carl Sandburg*, 1996, p. 110.

129 Sandburg, Carl. *The Complete Poems of Carl Sandburg*, 1969, p. 143.

130 Ibid., p. 624.

131 Sandburg, Carl. *Home Front Memo,* 1943, p. 85.

132 Ibid., p. 85.

133 Niven, Penelope. *Carl Sandburg: A Biography*, 1991, p. 546.

134 Sandburg, Carl. *Home Front Memo*, 1940, p. 192.

135 Ibid., p. 59.

136 Ibid., p. 45.

137 Ibid., p. 50.

138 Niven, Penelope. *Carl Sandburg: A Biography*, 1991, p. 561.

139 Golden, Harry. *Carl Sandburg*, 1961, p. 26.

140 Sandburg, Carl. *The Complete Poems of Carl Sandburg*, 1969, p. 646.

141 Golden, Harry. *Carl Sandburg*, 1961, p. 26.

142 Sandburg, Carl. *The Complete Poems of Carl Sandburg*, 1969, p. 60.

143 Ibid., p. 60.

144 Ibid., p. 148.

145 Ibid., p. 209.

146 Sandburg, Carl. *Breathing Tokens*, 1978, p. 149.

147 Niven, Penelope. *Carl Sandburg: A Biography*, 1991, p. 365.

148 Ibid., p. 394.

149 Ibid., p. 374.

150 Ibid., p. 363.

151 Ibid., p. 374.

152 Sandburg, Carl. *Rootabaga Stories*, 1922, p. 44.

153 Ibid., p. 5.

154 Ibid., p. 195.

155 Sandburg, Carl. *Rootabaga Stories*, 1922, p. 113.

156 Sandburg, Carl. *Rootabaga Pigeons*, 1923, p. 173.

157 Sandburg, Carl. *Rootabaga Stories*, 1922, p. 62.

158 Ibid., p. 79.

159 Ibid., p. 40.

160 Sandburg, Carl. *Rootabaga Pigeons*, 1923, p. 66.

161 Ibid., p. 176.

162 Ibid., p. 20.

163 Sandburg, Carl. *Rootabaga Stories*, 1922, p. 20.

164 Sandburg, Carl. *Rootabaga Pigeons*, 1923, p. 98.

165 Sandburg, Carl. *Rootabaga Stories*, 1923, p. 32.

166 Ibid., p. 10.

167 Ibid., p. 30.

168 Ibid., p. 53.

169 Ibid., p. 6.

170 Ibid., p. 6.

171 Ibid., p. 6.

172 Ibid., p. 62.

173 Ibid., p. 62.

174 Ibid., p. 82.

175 Ibid., p. 83.

176 Sandburg, Carl. *Rootabaga Pigeons*, 1923, p. 147.

177 Sandburg, Carl. *The Sandburg Range*, 1953, p. 113.

178 Sandburg, Carl. *The Complete Poems of Carl Sandburg*, 1969, p. 654.

179 Ibid., p. 656.

180 Ibid., p. 306.

181 Ibid., p. 655.

182 Durnell, Hazel. *The America of Carl Sandburg,* 1965, p. 28.

183 Sandburg, Carl. *The Complete Poems of Carl Sandburg*, 1969, p. 412.

184 Sandburg, Carl. *Potato Face* , 1930, p. ii.

185 Sandburg, Carl. *The Complete Poems of Carl Sandburg*, 1969, p. 210.

186 Sandburg, Carl. *The Sandburg Range,* 1957. p.34.

187 Ibid., p. 347.

188 Sandburg, Carl. *The Complete Poems of Carl Sandburg*, 1969, p. 320.

189 Sandburg, Carl. *Abraham Lincoln: The Prairie Years and The War Years,* 1954, p. 8.

190 Ibid., p. 8.

191 Niven, Penelope. *Carl Sandburg: A Biography*, 1991, p. 529.

192 North, Callahan. *Carl Sandburg: Lincoln of Out Literature*, 1960, p. 153.

193 Durnell, Hazel. *The America of Carl Sandburg*, 1965, p. 44.

194 Villarreal, Evert. *Recovering Carl Sandburg: Politics, Prose, and Poetry After 1920*, 2006, p. 89.

195 Niven, Penelope. *Carl Sandburg: Adventures of a Poet*, 2003, p. 9.

196 Niven, Penelope. *Carl Sandburg: A Biography*, 1991, p. 424.

197 Ibid., p. 433.

198 Durnell, Hazel. *The America of Carl Sandburg*, 1965, p. 182.

199 Haas, Joseph and Lovitz, Gene. *Carl Sandburg: A Pictorial Biography*, 1967, p. 134.

200 Detzer, Karl, *Carl Sandburg: A Study in Personality and Background*, 1941, p. 126.

201 Sandburg, Carl. *The Sandburg Range*, 1953, p. 459.

202 Villarreal, Evert. *Recovering Carl Sandburg: Politics, Prose, and Poetry After 1920*, 2006, p. 109.

203 Ibid., p. 84.

204 North, Callahan. *Carl Sandburg: Lincoln of Out Literature*, 1960, p. 135.

205 Golden, Harry. *Carl Sandburg*, 1961, p. 185.

206 Heitman, Danny. "A Workingman's Poem," 2013.

207 North, Callahan. *Carl Sandburg: Lincoln of Out Literature*, 1960, p. 84.

208 Villarreal, Evert. *Recovering Carl Sandburg: Politics, Prose, and Poetry After 1920*, 2006, p. 104.

209 Durnell, Hazel. *The America of Carl Sandburg*, 1965, p. 212.

210 Poetry Foundation. "Carl Sandburg."

211 Niven, Penelope. *Carl Sandburg: A Biography*, 1991, p. 680.

212 Sandburg, Carl. *Home Front Memo*, 1940, p. 3.

213 Durnell, Hazel. *The America of Carl Sandburg*, 1965, p. 219.

214 Niven, Penelope. *Carl Sandburg: A Biography*, 1991, p. 680.

215 Durnell, Hazel. *The America of Carl Sandburg*, 1965, p. 216.

216 Stepko, Barbara. "Marilyn Monroe and Carl Sandburg – An Unlikely and Intriguing Friendship," 2021, p. 1.

217 Ibid., p. 1.

218 Niven, Penelope. *Carl Sandburg: A Biography*, 1991, p. 366.

219 Ibid., p. 374.

220 Ibid., p. 374.

221 Bernstein, Arnie. *The Movies Are: Carl Sandburg's Film Reviews and Essays, 1920–1928*, 2000. p. vii.

222 Ibid., p. 76.

223 Ibid., p. 76.

224 Ibid., p. 69.

225 Ibid., p. 78.

226 Ibid., p. 204.

227 Niven, Penelope. *Carl Sandburg: A Biography*, 1991, p. 375.

228 Sandburg, Carl. *The Complete Poems of Carl Sandburg*, 1969. p. 302.

229 Niven, Penelope. *Carl Sandburg: A Biography*, 1991, p. 631.

230 Ibid., p. 632.

231 Ibid., p. 632.

232 Niven, Penelope. *Carl Sandburg: A Biography*, 1991, p. 177.

233 Ibid., p. 177.

234 Perry, Lilla S. *My Friend Carl Sandburg: The Biography of a Friendship*, 1981, p. 29.

235 D'Alessio, Gregory. *Old Troubadour: Carl Sandburg with his Guitar Friends*, 1987, p. 7.

236 Ibid., p. 7.

237 Ibid., p. 48.

238 Perry, Lilla S. *My Friend Carl Sandburg: The Biography of a Friendship*, 1981, p. 13.

239 Ibid., p. 65.

240 Durnell, Hazel. The America of Carl Sandburg, 1965, p. xi.

241 D' Alessio, Gregory. *Old Troubadour: Carl Sandburg with his Guitar Friends*, 1987, p. 9.

242 Perry, Lilla S. *My Friend Carl Sandburg: The Biography of a Friendship*, 1981, p. 120.

243 Ibid., p. 13.

244 Ibid., p. 120.

245 Niven, Penelope. *Carl Sandburg: A Biography*, 1991, p. 658.

246 Perry, Lilla S. *My Friend Carl Sandburg: The Biography of a Friendship*, 1981, p. 12.

247 Niven, Penelope. *Carl Sandburg: A Biography*, 1991, p. 462.

248 D'Alessio, Gregory. *Old Troubadour: Carl Sandburg with his Guitar Friends*, 1987, p. 106.

249 Ibid., p. 94.

250 Ibid., p. 95.

251 Niven, Penelope. *Carl Sandburg: A Biography*, 1991, p. 652.

252 Ibid., p. 652.

253 Niven, Penelope. *Carl Sandburg: A Biography*, 1991, p. 638.

254 Golden, Harry. *Carl Sandburg*, 1961, p. 171.

255 Sandburg, Carl. *The Complete Poems of Carl Sandburg*, 1969. p. 643.

256 Villarreal, Ebert. *Recovering Carl Sandburg: Politics, Prose, and Poetry After 1920*, p. 24.

257 Niven, Penelope. *Carl Sandburg: A Biography*, 1991, p. 610.

258 Ibid., p. 609.

259 *The Atlantic*, "Those Who Make Poems," 1942.

260 The American Presidency. "President Johnson Speech at Sandburg Memorial."

Index

P

pacifism, 67–68

Panic of 1893, 6, 23

paw-paws, 25, 28

Perry, Lilla S., 110–115

poems

"The Abracadabra Boys,"
119–120

"Anna Imroth," 34

"Arithmetic," 85

"Autumn Movement," 63

"Baby Toes," 75–76

"Bluebeard," 64–65

"Chicago," 14

"Child of the Romans," 35

"Daybreak," 63

"Doors," 84

"Falltime," 63

"Fog," 64

"The Four Brothers," 70

"Good Morning America,"
87

"Grass," 69

"The Guitar," 52

"Helga," 76

"Hydrangeas," 65

"Ice Handler," 35

"Iron," 69

"Is There Any Easy Road to
Freedom," 70–71

"Killers," 69

"The Man With Broken
Fingers," 71

"Mill-Doors," 13

"A Million Young
Workmen, 1915," 68

"New Farm Tractor," 23

"People With Chins," 86

"Prairie," 64

"Primer Lesson, 84–85

"The Road and the End," 7

"The Rooms," 24

"Second Sonata for Karlen
Paula," 76

"Singing ****," 54–55

"Skyscraper," 35

"Smoke," 69

"Stars," 63

"And They Obey," 69

"They Will Say," 34

"The Unknown War,"
73–74

"The Walking Man of
Rodin," 62

"Without the Cane and
the Derby (For C.C.),"
105

"Young Sea," 64

poetry, nature themes in,
63–65

Poor Writers Club, 9

prairie grass, 87

Presidential Medal of Freedom,
119

Progressive Era, 11

Pulitzer Prize, 95, 117

R

race relations, 36–40, 101, 104

recordings, 47–48, 53, 78

Roosevelt, Franklin Delano,
45–46, 53

About the Author

Dr. John W. Quinley, a retired college administrator and faculty member, was raised in Maywood Illinois—just a few blocks from where Sandburg had lived thirty years earlier. He directed planning and institutional research offices for a graduate school, a national association, and community colleges in four states. He taught classes in history, government, and humanities and currently works as an adjunct instructor for American History for Asheville-Buncombe Technical Community College in North Carolina. John holds an EdD in Higher Education Administration and an MA in Humanities.

Dr. Quinley served as a docent for Carl Sandburg Home National Historic Site for several years, and writes articles and gives presentations about Sandburg. He and his wife, Melissa, live in Hendersonville, North Carolina—just a few miles from Sandburg's former home.

Made in the USA
Columbia, SC
21 September 2022